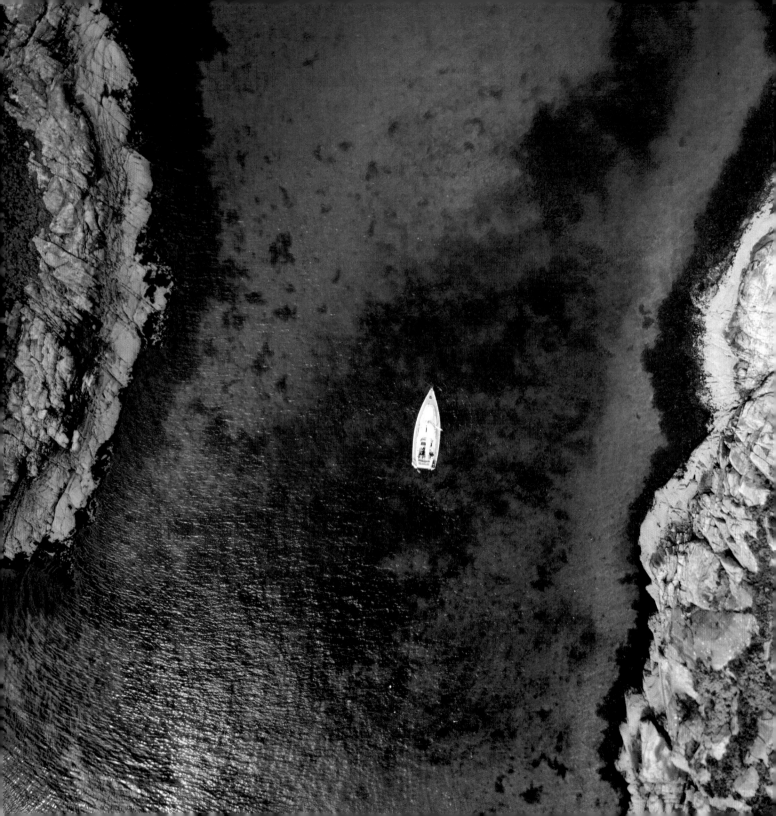

AROUND THESE ISLANDS IN **12 PORTS**

EXPLORING MARITIME BRITAIN AND IRELAND BY SAIL

JONATHAN WINTER

In association with:

In support of:

www.12ports.com

◀ *Loch Nevis anchorage*

Published by
Words by Design Ltd,
Bicester,
OX26 6HT
www.wordsbydesign.online

ISBN: 978-1-909075-96-2 (hardback)
e-ISBN: 978-1-909075-98-6 (ePub refloweable for small screens)
e-ISBN: 978-1-909075-97-9 (fixed format for large screens)
e-ISBN: 978-1-909075-99-3 (MOBI for Kindle)
First edition 2020

Acknowledgements
For the Islands I Sing: An Autobiography by George Mackay Brown copyright (c) George Mackay Brown, 2008. Reproduced with permission of Birlinn Limited through PLSclear.
Requests for permission via www.12ports.com

Print production: Words by Design
Editorial services: Kirsten Etheridge, Margaret Milton
Design: Jacqui Crawford Design
Technical illustration: Jules Birch

A catalogue record for this book is available from the British Library

Printed and bound in the UK by PODWW

ABOUT JONATHAN WINTER

Jonathan is a social entrepreneur and lifelong cruising sailor. He holds an RYA/MCA Yachtmaster Offshore qualification and a degree in aeronautical engineering, which fuels his interest in new boat designs. He and Anne live in Oxford and sail GT35-01, first of the GT yachts, designed by Stephen Jones.

www.linkedin.com/in/winter

ABOUT THESE ISLANDS

Founded in 2017, think tank These Islands believes in the value of the Union that is the United Kingdom. As a "forum for debate", they carry out research to enable open, well-informed discussion about the plural identities of the people of these islands.

www.these-islands.co.uk

ABOUT THE MISSION TO SEAFARERS

Founded in Bristol in 1835, The Mission to Seafarers provides practical, emotional and spiritual support to the 1.5 million crewmen and women who face danger every day to keep trade moving and economies afloat. The Mission operates through its network of chaplains and Seafarers Centres in over 50 countries.

www.missiontoseafarers.org

ACKNOWLEDGEMENTS

Take a summer off and sail round Britain? In less than two years, what seemed like a crazy idea turned into a practical plan. Many people deserve thanks for that. A brief boat-show chat with Tom Cunliffe encouraged us, as we browsed sailing books and bought Sam Steele's *UK and Ireland Circumnavigator's Guide*. That proved an invaluable source of data and confidence. At the time, our only boat was a 17-foot wooden skiff – beautiful but rather inadequate. But by the summer of 2018 – with one year to go – we found ourselves the stewards of a sleek, modern "Category A" cruising yacht, which we named *Nova*. Thanks to Conrad Cockburn (www.GTyachts.com), Stephen Jones (designer) and all the former team at Windboats who built her. Their help and encouragement made all the difference. Sam Taylor at These Islands, and podcast guru Catriona Oliphant, added an extra dimension and motivation to explore and discover in greater depth. Fourteen wise authors contributed the 12 articles. Marine artist Peter Kent conjured up sketches for the book, and told us stories. En route we were spurred on by fellow circumnavigators Jim and Angela aboard yacht *Shearwater*, and later by Nigel and Sue on *Serendipity*. Thanks also to our 22 crew, and to friends and family at home, particularly my parents, and my sister Kirsten Hall who acted as our emergency contact. Finally special thanks to Rosemary McLean, Caroline Moorhouse and all my colleagues at The Career Innovation Company who encouraged me to seize the moment, take a sabbatical and live the dream. They are an inspiration to me, as they are to many.

The crew of Nova: Kirsten Hall, Sam Hall, Alan Sayles, Ruth Drake-Chapman, Rob Wendover, Emil Nye, Caroline Ray, Nigel Pearson, Ben and Sally Amos, Zander and Claire Nye, Gayle, Andy, Grace and Matthew McKemey, Nigel Eves, Dai Gibbison, Camilla Cathro, Ben Ralston, Tim Edmonds, Lucy Driver.

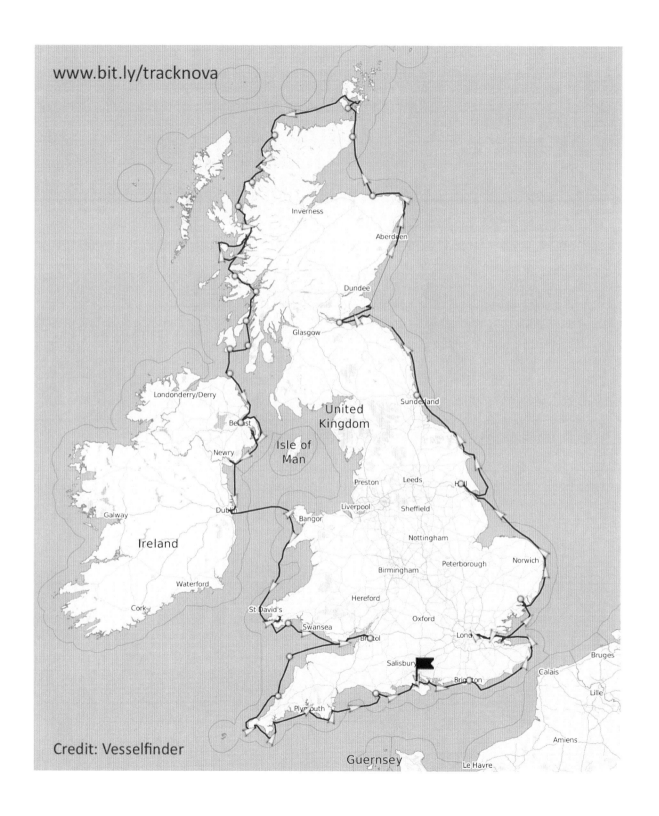

www.bit.ly/tracknova

Credit: Vesselfinder

CONTENTS

INTRODUCTION

PASSAGE
#AroundTheseIslands

STOPS
155 overnight stops

DISTANCE (NM)
2,587 (logged)

PASSAGE TIME (% +motor)
429h (45%)

WIND ON PASSAGE DAYS
F3 or less: 17 days
F6 or more: 9 days
The minimum and maximum
wind speed (Beaufort F0-8) and
direction (compass) are shown
in a "wind rose" diagram
for each leg of the voyage.

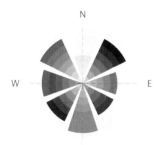

THIS BOOK FOLLOWS the voyage of yacht *Nova* around Britain in the summer of 2019. Sailed by Jonathan and Anne Winter with a total of 22 others joining as crew along the way, the itinerary encompassed 69 places over the course of 155 days, with *Nova* stopping in some for a week or more. The distance logged was 2,587 nautical miles (about 3,000 statute miles, or 4,800 kilometres).

The purpose of the journey was about more than sailing; it was to experience and learn about the places and people of these islands, at a time of national turmoil. It was to understand and to celebrate coastal towns and cities, whose trading relationships have, through history, defined our identity. Often these are places that have lived through tumultuous cycles of decline and reinvention, such as fishing ports. What makes some succeed while others continue to struggle? Would the differences and divisions laid bare by Brexit be obvious? Would there be hopeful or uniting themes?

Rather than taking the shortest route, wherever possible *Nova* therefore sailed up estuaries and rivers to the centre of cities, relishing the experience of arriving by sea. Twelve ports were chosen for more detailed exploration. They were selected for their significance, diversity and – more practically – equal spacing on the journey.

To bring depth to the project, we explored them in partnership with Catriona Oliphant (Chrome Media) who recorded podcasts, and with These Islands, a think tank, who gathered the 12 articles that form the basis of this book.

For the yacht's British designers, the voyage was also an opportunity to prove the "Grand Tour" credentials of their new kind of ocean-cruising vessel, the GT35, of which *Nova* is the first.

DEPARTURE

WISPS OF SEA smoke rose from the Beaulieu River as we got up with the sunrise on Easter Sunday morning. The sound of curlews, geese and even the occasional peacock are familiar here in the New Forest. It's a peaceful setting. Yet three miles away lies the oil refinery at Fawley, and it is just six miles from the bustling port and city of Southampton. Perhaps this juxtaposition of industry, history and landscape would be a foretaste of the experience of sailing around these islands.

The marina at Buckler's Hard was our place of departure. It's a historic place. In Napoleonic times, grand warships were built here. In World War II, D-Day preparations took place here. In sailing circles it is famed as the home of Sir Frances Chichester's yacht *Gypsy Moth IV*, in which he completed the first solo circumnavigation of the world.

We hosted a "casting-off party" for 40 people at the Master Builder's hotel – a rather grand gesture for such a relatively modest voyage. Yet, although modest in scale, the British coast and weather needs to be treated with great respect. Later we met a couple who said that sailing round the British coast was more challenging than anywhere else in their own four-year voyage round the world. Anyway, it was a good excuse for a party. Family, friends and collaborators visited *Nova* in warm sunshine over the weekend, and waved us off as we motored down the windless river, against the rising tide.

1. Easter morning on the Beaulieu River

2-4. Good excuse for a "casting-off party"

Setting out in very gentle conditions with novice crew, the journey ahead of us felt unreal. We really didn't know what lay ahead. We had prepared the boat immaculately and taken six months' sabbatical – more time than most. But were we ourselves prepared? Did we have the stamina and skill? Under the surface I carried a fear of incidents and accidents that would go beyond my capabilities. Yet the dream was vivid and drove us on. In my mind's eye there were towns, cities and wild anchorages all around the coast. I longed for the remote, out-of-reach places I had never been.

In the Solent heading east, we were keen not to put a dent in anything or anyone on day one. Fortunately Easter Sunday was quiet. In the summer these waters can be some of the busiest in the UK; dinghies, yachts, motorboats and personal watercraft buzz up and down. They make an uneasy mix with fast ferries and vast container and cruise ships, each with a 1000 m exclusion zone ahead of them, as they go to and from the first of our chosen ports: Southampton.

▶ *Port of Southampton handles around 14 million tonnes of cargo each year, and supports 15,000 jobs*

THE INVISIBLE SEA

MATT KERR

THIS ESSAY IS about not seeing the sea. Or about how to see the sea while not seeing it, taking as a particular case study Southampton in the 19th century.

By the Victorian period, Southampton's primary boast as a port was the speed with which things might depart from it – the city called itself the "Gateway to Empire", and it was part of its attractiveness that goods and people could move through without friction. Fruit arriving from South Africa in the morning could be in London markets by afternoon. It is indicative that when the railway came to Southampton in the 1840s, a tunnel was built from the ports, under the city, to the station so that gold bullion arriving from mines abroad could pass through the city without ever touching it.

Things might once have gone another way. Southampton was always a valuable seaport, in part because of the harbour's unique double tide, which is why legend suggests it as the place where King Cnut sat when making his vain attempt to hold back the waves. But, at the turn of the 19th century, Southampton seemed to offer more than a convenient point of entry or departure. In fact, John Feltham's *A Guide to All the Watering and Sea-Bathing Places* (1803) emphasised the variety of Southampton's attractions. Southampton was, Feltham claimed, "equally adapted for health, pleasure, and commerce", "uncommonly striking", and "almost unparalleled

Legend suggests it as the place where King Cnut sat when making his vain attempt to hold back the waves

in the beauty of its features". Such mixed purposes could be an advantage: precisely this combination of pleasure and commerce drew Jane Austen and her family, for example, to Southampton between 1806 and 1809, when the port was both fashionable and close enough to Portsmouth that her brother Frank could commute to work, as it were, in the navy.

Even for Feltham, though, Southampton seemed to lack something.

As a sea-bathing place, indeed, it has less reputation than some others that are described in this work. It has no machines, nor is its beach favorable for immersion; the marine is, also, deeply mixed with the fresh water.... The air is soft and mild, and sufficiently impregnated with saline particles to render it agreeable, and even salutary, to those who cannot endure a full exposure to the sea, on a bleak and open shore.

The sea at Southampton isn't quite the sea, its "saline particles" attenuated by the riverine atmosphere. The shift in register towards the end of this passage indicates that Southampton's aesthetics are, for Feltham, as mixed up as its atmosphere and water – instead of "full" exposure to marine sublimity, only a partial one is available, with the "bleak and open shore" adulterated by the miscellaneousness of Southampton's commitments to the sea. The initial comprehensiveness of Feltham's praise turns out to be a mixed blessing.

Compare the impressions of another Romantic visitor. The Isle of Wight, just off Southampton

Water, was the scene of composition of Keats's sonnet "On the Sea" (1817), which begins, "It keeps eternal whisperings around / Desolate shores", and enjoins the reader midway through: "O ye! who have your eye-balls vexed and tired, / Feast them upon the wideness of the Sea." In fact, it may have been Southampton itself that "vexed and tired" Keats: when he visited Southampton on the way to the Isle of Wight, he found little to hold his interest.

> I know nothing of this place but that it is long—
> tolerably broad—has bye streets—two or three
> Churches—a very respectable old Gate with
> two Lions to guard it. The Men and Women do
> not materially differ from those I have been in
> the Habit of seeing.... The Southampton water
> when I saw it just now was no better than a low
> Water Water which did no more than answer
> my expectations.

FROM A LETTER TO HIS BROTHERS DATED 15 APRIL 1817

Distant aesthetically, if not literally, from the bracing caverns and shores of the Isle of Wight, Southampton seemed to Keats an exemplar of the habitual and mundane, and disappointed him by meeting his expectations so unerringly.

Visual artists, too, have at times found in Southampton a challenging subject. J. M. W. Turner did a series of sketches in 1827 while watching the Cowes Regatta, but these failed to produce a finished artwork. James McNeill Whistler did paint Southampton. His *Nocturne: Blue and Gold – Southampton Water* (1872) was one of the first of his ekphrastic pictures, reconceiving as it does the view of the harbour as a musical form. Yet the ordering of his title may also suggest that, to Whistler, the specifics of place are subordinate to considerations of style and tint – and the artist has been taken at his word by the painting's holding institution, the Art Institute of Chicago, which interprets the image thus: "Although the work is based on his experience of the location, the specifics of place are inconsequential."

J. M. W Turner did a series of sketches in 1827 while watching the Cowes Regatta, but these failed to produce a finished artwork

Recently, a number of critics have emphasised the sea's invisibility as instrumental to its function in modernity. John Urry, for instance, writes that oceans "assemble as secret what would otherwise be onshore and visible", while according to Allan Sekula, "The metropolitan gaze no longer falls upon the waterfront, and a cognitive blankness follows." These are theoretical comments, which may seem not to have concrete effects, but the issue is practical too since some of

the major crises associated with the sea take place not only in the context of, but as a function of, the sea not being seen.

Southampton offers a good vantage point from which to attend to these concerns. Since the late 19th century, it has become still more difficult to say to what degree the specifics of Southampton as marine inspiration might have mattered to Whistler, Keats or any of the other writers and artists mentioned here. This is because between 1892 (when the Royal Pier opened) and 1934 (when the New Docks opened) the Southampton seaside that Whistler saw, and that Keats and Austen would also have recognised, was gradually transformed into industrial space through a programme of land reclamation that completely erased the place as it had existed prior.

The Southampton seaside that Whistler saw… was gradually transformed into industrial space

Today, Southampton provides a useful model of the sea's invisibility in part because Southampton is a place that routinely escapes notice. It cannot conform to picturesque ideals of seaside towns: Southampton was bombed heavily during World War II, and hurriedly rebuilt. It is a major cruise terminal, but not a destination for tourists. You would never know, but it is the primary point of entry for cars and trucks shipped from overseas. Across Southampton Water, the Fawley refinery supplies 20 per cent of the United Kingdom's oil – much of it invisibly, by direct pipeline. The docks are inaccessible to the public, and no bathing is possible in the city itself. But if the sea in Southampton is now more or less practically invisible, its invisibility is part of a longer history of British travel to the seaside, where anticipation and reality, the health-giving and the overwhelming, the particular and the general, have often met to obscure the specific qualities of even the most significant of seaside places.

A place that routinely escapes notice…. You would never know, but it is the primary point of entry for cars and trucks shipped from overseas

MATT KERR

Dr Matthew P. M. Kerr is a lecturer in British literature from 1837 to 1939 at the University of Southampton. Matt's research and teaching centre on Victorian literature and culture. His work spans both well-known figures – Dickens, Mill, Ruskin – and neglected ones, such as Captain Marryat. His articles have appeared in Essays in Criticism, Review of English Studies *and* Dickens Studies Annual, *amongst other places.*

Matt co-edited Coastal Cultures of the Long Nineteenth Century, *published in 2018 by Edinburgh University Press.*

SOLENT FORTS.COM

TO LONDON

PASSAGE
Southampton (Beaulieu)
to London (St Katharine Docks)

STOPS
Portsmouth
Brighton
Dover
Ramsgate
Thurrock

DISTANCE *(NM)*
238

PASSAGE TIME *(% +motor)*
37h (62%)

WIND

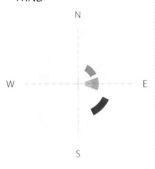

I TWAS DARK. We were tired at the end of a long day fighting the tide up the Thames and had just climbed into bed. Suddenly there was an eerie unnatural grinding noise on the hull, which grew louder and louder. We recognised the underwater noise of a propeller, but this time the volume was at a different magnitude. I jumped up and looked outside as a huge vessel passed close by on its way down the Thames. I would need to contain my curiosity in future to get any sleep. This was our first night near a major port, thanks to the friendly Thurrock Yacht Club, who lent us a mooring. It was one of our few potential stop-off points in the Thames Estuary on the way into central London.

The scale and scope of commercial traffic has been one of the revelations of this voyage, reminding us that almost all of our "stuff" comes by sea. Listening constantly on the marine VHF radio reveals a hidden world. Ships' captains with Russian accents are followed by the brief banter of Cockney tug boats, all coordinated by VTS (Vessel Traffic Service – the port authorities) in refined ex-naval tones. Without exception the interactions are professional, efficient and extraordinarily respectful. After a while I found myself joining in with "Sir" and "Ma'am".

1

2

1. Night mooring near Tilbury Docks

2. London's Cruise Terminal where The *SS Empire Windrush* arrived in 1948

3. Snaking past the O2 arena (Greenwich) en route to the City of London

Central London lived up to all expectations. We stayed in St Katharine Docks, designed by Thomas Telford and opened in 1828 to handle more goods and faster than any other dock in the world. Now it's a quiet haven. We were the only British visitors at the time, enjoying two peaceful nights, and meeting Catriona to record the first interview for the London podcast. Next morning before breakfast I jogged into the city, which was teeming with commuters. How could anyone convey London in a single article or podcast, I wondered? Impossible of course. But of all its characteristics, London's diversity is one of its greatest strengths, as the story of the Canvey Island Charedim conveys.

PILOT BOOKS
Imray – The Shell Channel Pilot
Imray – East Coast Pilot

ONLINE/APPS
www.visitmyharbour.com

▶ *London's city skyline includes Richard Rogers-designed "inside-out" Lloyds building*

THE CANVEY ISLAND CHAREDIM

DANIEL SUGARMAN

WHEN CANVEY ISLAND first began to be mentioned in connection with a potential new community of strictly Orthodox Jews, more than a few eyebrows were raised.

The challenges seemed considerable. For one thing, there was no extant pre-existing Jewish infrastructure – no synagogue, no mikvah (ritual immersion bath) and no easy access to kosher food.

Another thought that may have crossed a few people's minds was the area's political geography. Canvey is the hardest-of-hard Brexit country – with some of the pro-Brexit rhetoric about foreigners coming to Britain, what would the reaction be to a sudden influx of people whose dress and adherence to strict religious rules is decidedly "foreign"?

Canvey is the hardest-of-hard pro-Brexit country… what would the reaction be to a sudden influx of people whose dress and adherence to strict religious rules is decidedly "foreign"?

But according to Joel Friedman, a spokesperson for the Canvey Orthodox community, the three years since the community was established have been "brilliant – we've had very few problems".

As he put it, "There are always going to be haters, but we try to make the average Joe Bloggs on the street aware of who and what we are. We understand we look different, sometimes speak a different language [Yiddish], but we are trying to reassure them that we are not here to take them over. If they have any questions, they can come up and ask, and many of them do.

"If there's any problem, we will always try to nip it in the bud and always look for ways we can integrate. I tell them, 'There's many things we can't do, but there's so many more things we can do together.'"

Chris Fenwick, "born and bred" on Canvey, runs an inn on the island. The avuncular gentleman, who featured prominently in a BBC documentary about the arrival of the strictly Orthodox in the area, has become an unofficial intermediary between the Jewish newcomers and the other islanders.

"There's one thing I've learned about the people of Canvey Island – they are welcoming of strangers," he says.

As he points out, Canvey is far less homogeneous than people might think.

"When I was born here 65 years ago, there were 8,000 people living here; now there are 45,000. The majority have come down in waves, 80 per cent of them from the east of London. So our community is made up of East and North Londoners.

"We've got different groups, we've got Muslim groups that have been on Canvey for decades, for many years we've had a lot of Czech doctors. We have got quite a big Romanian community – and if you walk into the local supermarket, it's not unusual to hear Russian or Lithuanian spoken."

Therefore, he said, when he first heard about the plans to set up an Orthodox Jewish community in the area, "My instinct was that it could work – they can only actually enhance the place."

The last few years have not been totally devoid of incidents. In one case, a youth performed a Nazi salute in front of an Orthodox Jewish family. In another, a boy started mocking their mode of dress in front of them.

It's a problem all around the Home Counties, says Chris. "Youths cycling around bored, looking for trouble, fairly uneducated, unfortunately."

But on both occasions, says Chris, it was local people from Canvey who intervened and "straightened them out". In the former instance the police were involved in "re-educating" the boy involved.

Social media has also been a key tool in attempts to directly address concerns from local residents.

"There were rumours going around that we wanted to take over the area, build gates around it, that the men don't work and they're all on benefits – very stereotypical comments," Mr Friedman said.

"It's important to us to dispel those rumours and to get the truth out there, so that the normal people should understand what is going on. Let the haters hate."

It was 2016 when six strictly Orthodox Jewish families decided to take the plunge and move to the coast. The reason was simple: London's long-term housing crisis, which has affected few groups more acutely than the capital's strictly Orthodox community.

Charedim (the word, describing strictly Orthodox Jews, means "those who tremble" before God) tend to have far larger families than the societal norm. Statistically, this high birth rate means that strictly Orthodox Jews will make up the majority of the

UK's Jewish community before the end of the century.

When it comes to housing, however, that high birth rate can spell disaster. The largest community of Charedim in the UK – indeed, in Europe – is in Stamford Hill, a neighbourhood in North London straddling the boroughs of Hackney and Haringey. The local Jewish Orthodox housing association is highly competent, extremely hardworking – and completely oversubscribed, with many hundreds of families on its waiting list. Large houses in the area can cost in the region of a million pounds – totally unaffordable for such families. There are more than 250 marriages taking place within the Stamford Hill Jewish community every year. The housing situation was – and still is – unsustainable.

"I was one of the luckier ones," reflects Mr Friedman.

It was 2016 when six strictly Orthodox Jewish families decided to take the plunge and move to the coast. The reason was simple: London's long-term housing crisis

"I had rented a home; I had a three-bedroom terrace house with a garden, a lot of people don't even have that. People are holed up in flats and basements. [For] a lot of people, even if they have their own homes or are renting, the houses aren't necessarily the correct size for their family. People sometimes have six or seven children at home or more."

Mr Friedman, who was in the first group to move, described how a planning committee had looked at over a dozen different options, including the Essex island, and that although cheaper – and larger – housing had been a priority, of equal importance was proximity to London.

"About an hour's journey by car was the limit," he said.

"There are cheaper housing options than Canvey, in both Manchester and Gateshead [where there are already sizeable strictly Orthodox communities]."

The reason there has not been a full-scale move northwards is simple: "People aren't ready to give up their family connections and move somewhere with a different mentality and different services to London.

"Canvey is looked at as a satellite community, attached to London, and that's what people were looking for. A lot of people from the community in Canvey work in London, and vice versa; people come from London and provide services in Canvey.

"Canvey is trying to be a model of coexistence, of human brotherhood. In this day and age, with everything going on in the world, we've all got to try and get on"

Manchester is obviously a completely different distance."

Canvey is far from the first attempt to establish a new Charedi community outside London – for example, projects were launched in the past to build communities in both Hemel Hempstead and Milton Keynes. But whereas both those projects failed, Canvey appears to be succeeding.

"We did a lot of research with people involved in previous initiatives as to why they failed," Mr Friedman said.

"But for me, it looks like the housing crisis was getting worse and worse over the years. Milton Keynes was going back almost 20 years ago – the housing crisis was bad, but wasn't as bad as it is now, so the push [to move] wasn't as strong then."

Since its humble beginnings, the Canvey strictly Orthodox community has grown to more than 60 families, which is, as Mr Friedman says, a "massive increase".

There is now a synagogue and a ritual bath, and a little kosher shop; the likelihood is that the larger the community grows, the more amenities will become available – already there is talk about the possibility of setting up a kosher bakery.

It's a virtuous circle; the more strictly Orthodox families move to Canvey, the larger the community there gets, and the more people struggling with Stamford Hill house prices begin to see moving eastwards as a viable option.

"We hope that Canvey is one of the initiatives and hopefully there will be many more in the future, because we can't keep growing at the same percentage," Mr Friedman says.

He also makes it clear that the Charedim are trying "to spread across Canvey, and not focus just on a single area, for two reasons. Number one, we have more choice of houses coming up for sale, the wider the area we go – but also to make it less threatening for the locals. We don't want any 'taking over the area' comments; we're trying to integrate into the local community, and [if] we spread out, it makes it easier."

What has become clear is that though the local Canvey residents have doubtless had to become used to Charedim, the Charedim have also had to adapt, and work more closely with their non-Jewish neighbours.

"In London where [Orthodox] people have such a self-sustaining community, they are often not forced to think outside the box, whereas in a smaller community, we have to think of others," Mr Friedman says.

"We always have to think of others, but here it is even more important."

Meanwhile, Mr Fenwick says that his involvement with the Charedim has been "a real education. Their commitment to family… quite frankly, they've strengthened my faith in humankind.

"Canvey is trying to be a model of coexistence, of human brotherhood. In this day and age, with everything going on in the world, we've all got to try and get on."

DANIEL SUGARMAN

Daniel Sugarman is Public Affairs Officer for the Board of Deputies of British Jews. At the time of writing, he was a journalist for The Jewish Chronicle, *covering topics including UK politics, the UK's Jewish community and its relationship with other minority groups in Britain. He tweets at @daniel_sugarman.*

Stories he worked on include the Inner North London coronial dispute with the Jewish and Muslim communities, the Orthodox Jewish struggle to come to terms with the presence of Jewish LGBT+ people, and the continuous efforts of British Jewish individuals and organisations to combat antisemitism coming from all sides of the social and political divide. He has also written about the need for the UK Jewish community to stand together in support of other minority groups experiencing hate in Britain.

TO HULL

PASSAGE
London (St Katharine Docks)
to Hull

STOPS
Medway (Sharfleet) ⚓
Ipswich
Harwich (River Stour)
Lowestoft

DISTANCE (NM)
285

PASSAGE TIME (% +motor)
46h (70%)

WIND

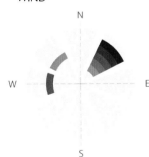

LEAVING LONDON THROUGH the Thames Barrier, we sailed out under the QEII bridge at Dartford, driven by our huge "Code Zero" sail past Canvey Island and eastwards. Darkness brought rain that night as we anchored alone in Sharfleet Creek on the Medway Estuary. In complete isolation we put on the lights and settled down to dinner.

The sound of another propeller broke the peace, and I poked my head out. There was a blue flashing light, and out of the gloom a fast RIB approached with dark-clad occupants. It reminded me of a time once when six heavily armed men in black approached us at speed in the Channel, in a similar boat. On that occasion they were Customs. "Are you Border Agency?" I asked. "No, we're Kent Police," they replied. Out on patrol until 2 a.m., an isolated yacht aroused their suspicion, so they came to investigate. Small boats around our coasts are one of the easiest ways for smugglers to bring drugs or people into the UK illegally, so it was reassuring to meet waterborne police. Surprisingly, this and a brief encounter on the Thames were the only two times we were questioned by the authorities on our entire journey.

We continued up the coast, past the skeletal wartime gun posts at Shivering Sands and Red Sands, skirting sandbanks and wind farms. Most of the time we were the only leisure craft in sight, except near Harwich. There we dodged squadrons of enthusiastic racing sailors, out in unreasonably strong winds over unfeasibly shallow waters.

1. The QEII Bridge, Dartford

2. Passing the Isle of Grain, towards the Medway Estuary

3. Red Sands Fort

We headed north again, past Galloping wind farm, one of 17 on the east coast. Today, the wind turbines were still and as we approached Lowestoft, fog descended. We motored through the chilly night, damp gathering on every surface of the boat and dripping down onto whoever was on watch. The instruments were lit up with commercial vessels. Occasionally we heard their engines but saw nothing.

Light dawned but the fog stayed with us until part-way up the Humber Estuary. Swept on by the tide and gentle breeze behind us, we reached Hull in the early afternoon, dropped the sails, crabbed the boat across the tide, executed a sharp turn and dived through the entrance into the still water beyond. It was a neat manoeuvre, but in a brief moment of satisfaction I let down my guard and *Nova* squelched to a halt on an unmarked muddy bank, to the amusement (I imagine) of two local boats who entered with us. We quickly freed ourselves, entered the lock and in a few minutes were tied up in prime position in the centre of the city of Hull.

PILOT BOOKS
Imray – East Coast Pilot

ONLINE/APPS
www.visitmyharbour.com

▶ *The Deep (aquarium) with Green Port Hull behind*

WOOL, WHALES AND WIND TURBINES

ROBB ROBINSON

THOUGH THE PLACE is some 25 or so miles up the Humber Estuary, Kingston upon Hull, or Hull as it is more commonly known, has always been psychologically orientated towards the sea. The broad brown-mud estuary is crucial to this unique port city's story. Its tributaries, and later canals, provided access to the heart of England, carrying goods to and from some of the powerhouses of the world's first industrial nation whilst, downstream, it provided a link to the rest of the world. The sea was the first world-wide web and for countless generations Hull people and ships have voyaged down the Humber on their way to do their business in great waters.

It was a busy place, a congested clutter of fine houses, humble dwellings, taverns, shops and warehouses

The oldest part of the port is the Old Town, founded by the monks of Meaux Abbey to dispatch wool, then the staple product of England's overseas trade. The early medieval settlement, which can still be discerned in the area's street layout, grew up where the western bank of the River Hull entered the great Humber Estuary. The lower reaches of lesser river are known as the Old Harbour and have long been home to a congregation of quays – known locally as staiths. Here countless generations of merchants conducted their commerce, transhipping at one time or another almost every kind of maritime cargo.

Just behind this waterfront is the High Street,

which winds its way along one side of an otherwise typical medieval gridiron of narrow lanes. This was the original main thoroughfare and follows the broadly north–south weave of the River Hull as it approaches the Humber Estuary. Much of the eastern side of this street was eventually fronted with fine merchant dwellings, behind which lay commodious warehouses and all-important private staiths. It was a busy place, a congested clutter of fine houses, humble dwellings, taverns, shops and warehouses. Even today, despite having confronted the combined ravages of the World War II Blitz and misguided post-war planning projects, the cobbled streets and ancient buildings of this tightly built area still convey somewhat of a scenically sea-stained essence of its maritime heyday and retain a number of these fine old houses and museums.

The port's first dock was built in the 1770s and when it was opened, it was the largest such facility in the country – nearly 11 acres, dug out by hand with pickaxe, shovel and wheelbarrow. It was followed by a series of other docks, following the line of Hull's old medieval walls. By 1830 the Old Town was an island bounded on every side by water – in some places by these docks and in others by the River Hull or the actual estuary of the Humber. Kingston upon Hull was granted city status in 1897 and in the early 20th century the port already stretched a long way beyond the confines of the medieval Old Harbour, having spread along the north bank of the great Humber Estuary. Seven miles of docks and warehouses fronted the Humber or the River Hull,

handling vast amounts of international trade. The commodities they handled were many and various, worked by lumpers and raff yard workers, deal porters, coal heavers and trimmers, corn porters and bobbers – the latter of whom unloaded fish.

Many famous ships were built in the port, not least the *Bethia*, better known as the *Bounty*. Others include the *Alexander*, part of the First Fleet to Australia, HMS *Boreas*, Nelson's long-time command in the West Indies, and HMS *Hecla*, the famous polar exploration ship used by Parry on four expeditions. Talking of all things polar, five members of Shackleton's famous 1914–1917 expedition were from or linked with Hull, more than from any other place, and a decade or so earlier, in 1902–4, Hull's Captain William Colbeck, with a crew consisting substantially of Hull seafarers aboard the ship *Morning*, played a crucial role in rescuing Scott and the *Discovery* when they were trapped by ice in the McMurdo Sound. During the 18th and early 19th centuries Hull was the largest whaling port in the country and its sailors had an unrivalled knowledge of Arctic waters. In the Great War, the steam trawler *Viola*, built to supply London with fish from the North Sea, was one of hundreds of Humber steam fishing vessels that were requisitioned and armed by the Admiralty. *Viola* sailed off from its home port with its crew of local trawlermen in September 1914; during more than four years of active service on the maritime front line, it sailed many more miles on patrol than any dreadnought, and was involved in numerous actions with enemy vessels and the

sinking of at least two U-boats. Now, one of only four ships left that saw action in the Great War, it has yet to return to its home port from that Great War voyage. Today *Viola* lies at the old whaling station of Grytviken in South Georgia after an eventful career that encompassed much of the long Atlantic Ocean; a Viola Trust has been formed in Hull to recover the vessel and hopefully return it to its home port. Indeed, ripple the surface of many stories of the sea and you will come across Hull people and ships.

We sometimes forget that by the early 20th century, when Britain was the largest and most powerful maritime nation in the world, Hull was already known as the country's Third Port. It was not only one of the world's leading fishing ports,

Many famous ships were built in the port... the Bounty... Nelson's HMS Boreas... Indeed, ripple the surface of many stories of the sea and you will come across Hull people and ships

its trawlers reaching as far afield as Iceland and the Barents Sea, but it was also of global significance in terms of trade and commerce. One of the most important Hull shipping firms of the Edwardian epoch was Thomas Wilson Sons & Co., which had become, according to *The Times*, the largest privately owned shipping company in the world. In 1917 the company was acquired by Hull-born Sir John Ellerman, often considered to be the richest person who has ever lived in Britain; for years afterwards, called Ellerman's Wilson Line, the company was a household name.

Because the port enjoyed many close connections with the Continent, it played a significant role in the great movement of peoples from Europe to the New World. Between 1840 and 1914 more than 2.2 million migrants passed through Hull en route to west-coast ports for onward voyages to America. Ellis Island in New York, the portal through which many of these migrants eventually entered the United States, is now a museum. In Hull this remarkable movement of people is marked with a statue close by the Humber.

In the 1982 Falklands War more Hull civilian ships were taken up for active Admiralty service than from any other British port

Large numbers of Hull seafarers and ships were lost during both world wars, and in the 1982 Falklands War more Hull civilian ships were taken up for active Admiralty service than were requisitioned from any other British port. During the Blitz, Hull probably suffered proportionally more bomb damage than any other British city. We are lucky that so much survived.

Though the city was adversely affected by the decline of the British shipping industry in the second half of the 20th century and by the loss of most of its once world-famous distant water fishing fleet after being on the wrong side of a series of Cod Wars with Iceland, it remains a resilient place. Time and again over the centuries, as town and city alike, its people have demonstrated an independence of spirit and outlook whilst at the same time making the most of opportunities offered across an ever-changing world. The modern city contains one of the most effective and efficient European ports and the ferries that ply daily between Hull and the Continent are amongst the largest and most modern to be found anywhere in the world. The recent arrival of the Siemens Gamesa turbine factory has added a significant new dimension to its maritime portfolio.

The modern city contains one of the most effective and efficient European ports

In 2009 Hull hosted the Clipper Round the World Yacht Race and in 2017 the place revelled in its UK City of Culture status, attracting visitors from far and wide. Today, commercial shipping is increasingly concentrated along the port's eastern waterfront, whilst the Old Town docks have been variously converted into great gardens, a striking shopping centre built on stilts in the water and spacious marinas. A walk around its streets and waterfront areas will reveal many hidden gems, not least Hull Trinity House, which this year celebrates 650 years since its foundation, and Wilberforce House on the ancient High Street, which was once home to the man who played such an important role in the abolition of slavery.

Hull lies in a landscape of huge skies, set amongst flat green fields many miles from other English cities. It is not at the end of the line as some landlubbers would tell you but is a portal to the wider world. It could be argued that over the epochs, Hull's distinctive geographical situation has permeated the attitudes and personalities of so many of its people and encouraged an independence of outlook, and a taste for freedom that has found an outlet in so many ways, not least in its unique white telephone boxes, its distinctive local dialect, by actions such as closing its gates on St George's Day 1642 to bar an authoritarian Charles I from the town – even before the start of the English Civil War – or in the many, many stories of individual lives of its townsfolk, particularly on the high seas.

Hull has a remarkable maritime history and yet remains an important player in the world of modern global maritime commerce. Building on the legacy of its 2017 City of Culture status, the place is set to make much more of its extensive and priceless maritime assets and singular global story through its recently announced Yorkshire's Maritime City Project, which, with Heritage Lottery Fund support, intends to transform the existing maritime museum and open up important waterfront assets –

including the port's historic ships – and to create new displays with the intention of swelling the increasing number of visitors who travel to this unique port city each year.

ROBB ROBINSON

Dr Robb Robinson is a maritime historian based at the Blaydes Maritime Centre, Hull, and an honorary research fellow of the University of Hull. He comes from a family steeped in the business of seafaring and the sea for generations and is the author of five books and numerous academic articles. His publications include Far Horizons: From Hull to the Ends of the Earth, *which is a collection of biographies of people and ships that have made a global impact, and he is one of the trustees of the Viola Trust, which seeks the return to the UK of one of the last surviving vessels that saw action in the Great War.*

TO DUNDEE

PASSAGE
Hull to Dundee (Arbroath)

STOPS
Filey Bay ⚓
Whitby
North Shields
Lindisfarne ⚓
Edinburgh (Port Edgar)
Pittenweem

DISTANCE *(NM)*
360

PASSAGE TIME *(% +motor)*
58h *(66%)*

WIND

DEPARTING FROM HULL just before high tide, we made fast progress down the Humber to Spurn Point. There we reported to VTS on the radio, crossed the shipping channel, sailed past the remote lifeboat station (the only one in the UK with full-time crew) and rounded the point close to the shingle at speed with a roaring tide under us.

With sun and a good breeze we sailed northwards confidently, but not fast enough, towards Flamborough Head. We had ignored local advice from two sailors in Hull, who advised leaving two hours earlier, against the tide. This was our first big tactical mistake of the voyage. Dodging wind farms and submerged pot buoys, we missed the "tidal gate" and found ourselves fighting against a stream of up to 3 knots. Thankfully we reached Filey Bay just before nightfall and dropped anchor. The next day, we reached Whitby.

Continuing up the east coast, we spotted all sorts of commercial vessels: bulbous tug boats, gigantic fishing trawlers, fast catamarans transporting wind-farm maintenance crew, and even an experimental high-speed wave-piercing crew transfer vessel (pictured) undergoing sea trials. Most wind-farm transfer boats dock bow-to against a wind turbine so their crew can climb the ladder. It's not a procedure they can carry out when the weather closes in – then they resort to helicopter transfer.

The most hi-tech boat was a small autonomous survey catamaran we saw twice in Scotland. This drone boat (www.xocean.com) is capable of 18 days and 1,500 miles at sea, controlled from an office in Ireland. On a different scale, the most extraordinary vessels were a pair of 130 m-long "Windcarrier" wind turbine transporters, *Brave Tern* and *Bold Tern*. These boats jack themselves up out of the water on stilts, clear of the waves, before planting a new turbine tower on the seabed. For us, they vividly conveyed the exciting new generation of maritime activity giving life to historic port cities like Hull and the Humber, and powering up the UK.

It was, however, the natural world that dominated our experience as we sailed. Seabirds in particular were our constant companions. We stopped at the Farne Islands, surrounded by thousands of guillemots and puffins in the sunshine, before anchoring for the night at Holy Island (Lindisfarne). There we also saw our first large-scale seal colony – a line of black along the beach.

1. Waiting for the swing bridge at Whitby

2. Crew transport vessel for wind farms

3. "Tenacity" - Experimental wave access vessel

Our unexpected wildlife "high" was on the approach to Edinburgh. It was raining gently as we rounded St Abb's Head and entered the Firth of Forth. Ahead of us was Bass Rock, rising steeply out of the sea. We knew nothing of it, and today it appeared to be smoking like a quietly active volcano. Closer, and we could see it was not smoke, but a haze of midges. Closer still, it was clearly a giant swarm of bees. Finally we realised this white-capped rock is in fact home to the world's largest colony of northern gannets – over 150,000 of them. I love gannets for their sleek perfection of design as flying and hunting creatures. I think of them in ones and twos, wheeling and diving. To see them in these numbers, flying to and fro carrying seaweed for their nests, and dotting the rock in vast numbers, felt like a world-scale wildlife treat. And there it was on the doorstep of Scotland's capital.

After a few days in Edinburgh, it was time to approach our fourth port. There's nowhere for a deep-draft yacht to moor in Dundee itself, so we berthed at nearby Arbroath and took the train into the city of Jam, Jute, Journalism and (these days) Joysticks: Dundee.

PILOT BOOKS
RNYC – Sailing Directions, Humber to Rattray Head

ONLINE/APPS
www.visitmyharbour.com

▶ *Desperate Dan – one of several DC Thomson characters depicted in the centre of Dundee*

COMINGS AND GOINGS

MICHAEL MARRA

ROWING BACK AGAINST the clock face, head north from the tattooists of Leith past the golf course and take your next left. As spring turns to summer and warming air cools on the North Sea waters, the cover of Haar brings you into the Tay estuary under a thick tumbling cloud. We will be waiting on the blurred north shoreline as you emerge. The people of Dundee will be further distracted by their June entertainment of Fife disappearing off the southern end of the earth while the sun bakes the slopes of the Law, warming the rasps on their canes and promising verdant afternoons of football in Balgay, Baxter, Caird and Lochee parks.

Steel ships would crack like rotten eggs in the winter ice

Dundee is "The Smiling School for Calvinists", as per Bill Duncan's joyful apocrypha. Duncan's tale of the Inuit fisherman is a quintessential port town watching of the comers and the goers; those who arrived and never left, people who came, blazed brightly and disappeared by night or by Haar. Caught first in the wake of the city whaler, capsized and towed south to the Tay, our Inuit friend is caught for a second time, and for years, by cellar-cooled pints of heavy in the sweating pubs of the Sinderins. And then he was gone.

The whalers brought money and trade as well as massive fatty fish to the Dundee seaboard. Dundee learned to build fine wooden ships that would endure the harshest of climates. Steel ships would crack like rotten eggs in the winter ice of the far southern oceans. Dundee ships, whittled from pitch pine, English elm and Guyana greenheart, could breathe yet in the Antarctic's ever tighter embrace: yielding slowly, finding space within themselves and hunkering down for the thaw. The trade routes that mattered – more Whelks Road than Silk Roads – were easterly to Scandinavia and Europe.

The Industrial Revolution changed everything, everywhere. Still the ships came, few whales and less linen, but now ever bigger and laden with jute for the looms. Trench warfare made for a booming sandbag market from Gettysburg to the Somme. The loose raw hemp of Indian fields flecked the air and lungs of the dockers and came with fabulous ballast: oranges, soul music, an elephant. We invented marmalade, begat the Average White Band and dissected Dumbo. The gold lettering of the shipping routes still adorns first floor windows. Calcutta. Kandahar. Bombay.

This hungry monoculture of jute mills drained the surrounding Angus glens of farmhands as the old city burgh boomed. The Irish walked barefoot in great numbers from famine in the west to loose

The loose raw hemp of Indian fields… came with fabulous ballast: oranges, soul music, an elephant. We invented marmalade…

their limbs in the looms. The beneficent barons donated those fine parks in return. Compensation for pittance wages, regular maiming, child labour and an early death. A few green fields did not quite cut it. Us Irish organised.

All this while, across the long 18th and 19th centuries, the British Isles were flipping upon their axis to face the Atlantic, leaving Scandinavia at our back. The comings and goings that mattered for Dundonians were now North and South. Instead of being our lifeline, our river became our obstacle, so we crossed it by building the longest bridge in the entire world. "A mighty long bridge for such a mighty little old town," opined Ulysses S. Grant as he arrived in 1876, perhaps to say thank you for the sandbags. Dundee marched away from the sea. Trains came and trains went.

The economic cycles of Dundee's history define our relationship to the world. The latest phase is of a new cool, real tourism and PR fluff. *Lonely Planet* say we are one of the best places in Europe to visit. *The Wall Street Journal* calls us the coolest city in Scotland. You would do well to compare the zeitgeist to the lived reality of increasing poverty levels, massive economic inactivity and public services that are chronically mismanaged as well as increasingly underfunded. Puff pieces in magazines will put some bread on the table but the potential of the tourist economy is insufficient to make a dent in the stark statistics. The centrepiece of all of this is the V&A Dundee, opened in 2018, which gathers ever more awards, and rightly so. It is spectacular and well worth your time. The project idea was dreamt up a decade ago by Professor Georgina Follett, then Dean of the

University of Dundee's College of Art & Design. The knowledge economy of higher education was to be the first-order beneficiary of the changed image of the city. The sense of post-industrial decline had long been a brake on the success of a university with justifiable global ambitions in the fields of design and life sciences.

The V&A's summer exhibition for 2019 appropriately reflects on the design of video games globally. Dundee produced the iconic ZX Spectrum personal computer in the Timex factory in the 1980s. The story goes that the availability of knock-off "speccies" available in city pubs for a couple of pounds enabled a generation of programmers more effectively than the code clubs and digital skills strategies of today. In any

Instead of being our lifeline, our river became our obstacle, so we crossed it by building the longest bridge in the entire world

Discovery at Dundee

case, the city brought forth *Lemmings* and *Grand Theft Auto*. In movie terms that's like a tiny studio in the Welsh valleys knocking out James Bond, *Star Wars* and *The Lord of the Rings*. The skills nurtured in this sector by the University of Abertay typifies the new industries that pay the kind of wages that Dundee needs. It also says something of the great displacement of the physical trade routes in favour of the frictionless digital as the focus of policy and practice for government and businesses.

The North Sea renewable industry and the decommissioning of aged oil infrastructure should, theoretically, provide an economic opportunity for the kind of blue-collar workers that still have little access to the knowledge economy. Dundee's greatest statistical outlier is male economic inactivity for the over forties. This is the human face and consequence of continued decline in Scottish manufacturing. Could a working river not provide opportunity as it once did? As long as turbines are manufactured thousands of miles away and on their way to the North Sea bypass rigs floating abroad to be broken up, the answer will be no. It is worth the fight though. Just Transition. Green New Deal. This is where the rubber hits the road. Or the prow cuts the breaking waves.

Claims that the constitutional twins of Brexit and another Scottish referendum can provide the "policy levers" for economic renewal dominate policy debate. For a decade now they have been to the detriment of progress and are driving decline.

You will do well to be away while the Haar has abated. Do not suffer the fate of General Monck's army and founder on the many shallow banks of the Tay's estuary. The booty of a long-sacked city rests in the silvery depths there. The real treasure was always our people and this place. Go slowly and take the sunset. Comings and goings. Leavers and remainers. Lost treasure to be found. Futures already written. Safe journey.

The Wall Street Journal calls us the coolest city in Scotland. You would do well to compare the zeitgeist to the lived reality of increasing poverty…

MICHAEL MARRA

Michael Marra (writing in a personal capacity) is the deputy director of research at the University of Dundee. He previously spent four years as Deputy Director of Design in Action – one of the AHRC's flagship Knowledge Exchange Hubs for the Creative Economy. Michael has published on industrial policy and the innovative mobilisation of intellectual property. His background in public policy and political affairs has included posts in the Scottish and UK Parliaments as a senior political adviser and as Head of Policy and Public Affairs for Oxfam. He is a graduate of the London School of Economics and Political Science and previously from the University of Glasgow, where he has taught international comparative politics. He is an elected member of Dundee City Council.

▶ *Royal Research Ship Discovery (1901) and the new V&A museum*

TO STROMNESS

PASSAGE
Dundee (Arbroath)
to Stromness

STOPS
Peterhead
Whitehills
Wick
Longhope
Hunda Sound ⚓

DISTANCE *(NM)*
238

PASSAGE TIME *(% +motor)*
36h (62%)

WIND

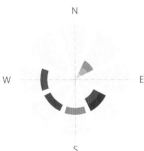

IF THIS JOURNEY were an ascent, the mountaintop would naturally be the Orkney Islands, and the last camp on the route would be Wick. We arrived there ahead of strong easterly winds, which might have prevented us from entering the harbour and sent us scuttling all the way back across the Moray Firth. The lifeboat crew were preparing for their Harbour Day. There's a good reason for lifeboats around here – the Pentland Firth has a fearsome reputation. The Admiralty Sailing Directions from 1935 says, "when a swell is opposed to the tidal stream, a sea is raised which can scarcely be imagined by those who have never experienced it".

Wick was a welcome surprise. Its large sheltered harbours and the town above were designed by Thomas Telford on instruction from Sir William Pulteney, governor of the British Fisheries Society. It became the world's largest herring port, with over 1,000 fishing vessels in the summer. Peak herring was in 1867 when it is said that 50 million "silver darlings" were gutted and packed in just two days by 3,500 herring lassies. To accommodate everyone, Telford also built Pulteneytown, an early planned town, partly modelled on Bath. Today this part of Wick is best known for its whisky.

Harbour Day dawned with unexpected fog, which lasted all day. Wind fluttered the colourful flags on all the boats, including *Nova*. The town turned out in force, and at the appointed time the Longhope

lifeboat loomed into view, visiting from Orkney. It was a solemn moment as the crowds commemorated the 50th anniversary of the disaster in which eight of the Longhope crew were lost. We met people whose relatives were amongst them. It was clear that an event like this further cements the pivotal role the lifeboats play in small coastal communities. We enjoyed generous hospitality from Mark, the lifeboat coxswain, and his team, who served barbecued steak marinated in cider and flamed in Old Pulteney, and partied into the night.

Next morning, time came for us to leave. We looked for Malcolm, the harbour master, who had promised advice, and found him clearing up after the party. "Head for Skirza," he said, "until you reach the 26 m contour. You'll find a back eddy along the shore to Duncansby Head. If you arrive there an hour before the tide turns north-west, you'll find the current will continue north across the Pentland Firth." He smiled at our nervous looks. "Follow my advice and you won't be troubled by the Firth. It will be 'oilies off, slippers on'." And so it was.

1. RNLI Harbour Day at Wick
2. 1895 herring boat *Isabella Fortuna*
3. *Nova* at Longhope, Orkney

1. Skuas and gannets in Switha Sound

2. Midsummer night light

3. Stromness Severn class lifeboat (10:30 p.m.)

Arriving in Scapa Flow, the wind rose and we tacked fast towards Longhope, passing a large flock of gannets and arctic skuas wheeling and diving with intent. We went ashore and visited our newly made lifeboat friends before returning to the boat in the late sun of midsummer's eve. The sun set at half past ten, and light never disappeared from the colourful sky.

Our time in Scapa Flow coincided with the 100th anniversary of the scuttling of the German fleet at the end of the Great War. Sailing across the flat waters towards Stromness, we could see why this has been a significant naval harbour. The tides around Orkney are notorious, but Scapa Flow is like the Solent – perfectly sheltered. We passed the ferry terminal and tied up in the small marina, ready to explore this place full of stories.

10.20pm
01.00am
03.30am
04.30am

PILOT BOOKS
RNYC – Sailing Directions,
    Humber to Rattray Head
Clyde Cruising Club –
    Sailing Directions, Orkney and
    Shetland Islands incl. N and
    NE Scotland

ONLINE/APPS
www.visitmyharbour.com

▶ Nova *(top LH berth) in the marina at Stromness*

MADE OF STORIES

NICK ISBISTER

STROMNESS, FROM THE Norse *Straumsnes*, means the "headland protruding into the tidal stream". The Vikings called it Hamnavoe: "peaceful" or "safe harbour". It is the second-most populous town in Orkneyjar (Old Norse for "Seal Islands").

Poet and novelist George Mackay Brown (GMB) lived there for much of his life, and in his poem "Hamnavoe" he sees it as the safe haven for "boats [that] drove furrows homeward, like ploughmen, in blizzards of gulls". GMB went away to Edinburgh for his education, but returned to Stromness to live, and love and write. He is buried there too. Composer Sir Peter Maxwell Davies, formerly Master of the Queen's Music, chose to live there, or thereabouts. It seems that Orkney holds a strange magnetism for those who encounter its storm-ridden, windswept, desolate charms. It finds its way into people's personal stories.

> *The universe is made of stories, not atoms*
>
> MURIEL RUKEYSER

MY STORY

At the age of 11 I learned that there was a set of islands just north of Scotland where there were many people with my name. Then I learned that 5,000 years ago at a place called Isbister there was a unique chambered tomb where humans were buried with the bones of 14 white-tailed sea eagles, now known as the "Tomb of the Eagles" – a chambered tomb on top of a dramatic cliff.

I was hooked. I was connected to a past; I had a distinctive heritage; I had a place I could think of as "where I'm from". I may not be living there, but my identity had roots, my name took me on the genetic path that is the equivalent of the stone path constructed as a timeline from the visitor centre at Skara Brae through the sand dunes all the way to the remarkable stone houses dating back to 3200 BC. That's a long, long path. The first man on the moon, the US Declaration of Independence, 1066, the fall of Rome, the birth of Christ, The Great Wall of China, the Pyramids, and still the path goes on. Of course, it is all a story, I tell myself, but that's the point: we are our stories. As poet Muriel Rukeyser put it: "The universe is made of stories, not atoms."

Far from being "off the beaten track", 5,000 years ago Orkney *was* the beaten track, and even in the 20th century this archipelago became central once again during the two world wars. In 1919 the German navy scuttled their fleet in Scapa Flow, a key naval centre.

The archaeologist in charge of the excavations at the Ness of Brodgar puts it like this:

> *Far from being off the beaten track… Orkney was the beaten track*

> *We need to turn the map of Britain upside down when we consider the Neolithic and shrug off our south-centric attitudes. London may be the cultural hub of Britain today, but 5,000 years ago, Orkney was the centre for innovation for the British isles. Ideas spread from this place.*

NICK CARD OF THE ORKNEY RESEARCH CENTRE FOR ARCHAEOLOGY

TRIUMPHS OF THE HUMAN SPIRIT

What an astonishing group of people committed themselves to create such monumental works as the Ring of Brodgar and the Stones of Stenness. When dedicated as a UNESCO World Heritage site in 1998 the commendation said:

The monuments at the heart of Neolithic Orkney and Skara Brae proclaim the triumphs of the human spirit in early ages and isolated places. They were approximately contemporary with the mastabas of the archaic period of Egypt (first and second dynasties), the brick temples of Sumeria, and the first cities of the Harappa culture in India, and a century or two earlier than the Golden Age of China. Unusually fine for their early date… these sites stand as a visible symbol of the achievements of early peoples away from the traditional centres of civilisation…The Ring of Brodgar is the finest known truly circular late Neolithic or early Bronze Age stone ring.

The Ness of Brodgar, the Stones of Stenness, the Ring of Brodgar, *all* constructed before the Pyramids. The archaeological evidence suggests that different parts of the henge were developed by different groups. Look what can be achieved when people commit to a common purpose, and vest something of their identity in something beyond mere subsistence. When people decide to assert their identity, whether to themselves or to "others" or, perhaps most pertinently to this enduring

monument, to something or someone or some many others (ancestors) beyond the here and now, it sends a powerful message.

VANDALS?

"Vandals deface historic monument." On 11 April 2019, just a few days before yacht *Nova* set out around these islands, the BBC ran these headlines: "Police are investigating vandalism at Orkney's Ring of Brodgar." The story continues:

Built 5,000 years ago, the Neolithic ceremonial site near Stenness is the third largest stone circle in the British Isles. Graffiti was scratched into one of the ring's 27 standing stones sometime between Friday afternoon and Sunday morning. Police Scotland described the stones as "priceless artefacts" and the vandalism as a "mindless act".

Look what can be achieved when people commit to a common purpose… to assert their identity

"Vandalism" – the activity of "vandals". Mindless, thoughtless Vandals. Maybe the Goths, and the Visigoths and the Vandals were more destructive than other invaders of ancient times – they certainly inspired John Dryden to write: "Till Goths, and Vandals, a rude Northern race / Did all the matchless Monuments deface." ("To Sir Godfrey Kneller", 1694).

The historic monuments of Orkney have repeatedly been the objects of such defacing. The Neolithic Chambered Tomb of Maeshowe houses one of the largest collections of runes outside Norway. According to the *Orkneyinga Saga*, a medieval "history" of the earls of Orkney, the runes were written by a group of Viking raiders who took refuge in the tomb from a storm. These are manifestly graffiti: "Ingebjork the fair widow – many a woman has walked stooping in here a very showy person" signed by "Erlingr"; "Thorni f*cked. Helgi carved" (most guidebooks substitute a more acceptable translation to this); "Ofram the son of Sigurd carved these runes"; "Haermund Hardaxe carved these runes".

If graffiti changed anything – it would be illegal

BANKSY

Are these mindless acts of vandalism, or are they assertions of individual identity? We treasure the Viking graffiti now; maybe we will never treasure the crude scrawls that were recently added to the stones at Bodgar. To suggest that they might not be mindless is not to endorse or condone them. But they can be framed in other ways. Certainly, Banksy would, as he daubed, "If graffiti changed anything – it would be illegal."

Interestingly, my visit to the Ring of Brodgar in 2001 left a profound impression on me, not least because in this astonishing assertion of collective identity, hidden away on one of the stones was some ancient graffiti – the name J Isbister, *my* name, with the date 1881. Whilst I am a great fan of Diana Gabaldon's *Outlander* TV series, I'm unconvinced that I travelled back in time to carve my name as a "mindless act of vandalism". But I do feel an astonishing sense of continuity, and indeed meaning for me in this simple piece of graffiti.

George Mackay Brown concludes his autobiography with these words:

… stories from under the horizon ought always to be welcome – and so they have been, in Orkney, for centuries: but they are never utterly new.

There are mysterious marks on the stone circle of Brodgar in Orkney, and on the stones of Skarabrae village, from 5,000 years ago. We will never know what they mean. I am making marks with a pen on paper, that will have no meaning 5,000 years from now. A mystery abides. We move from silence into silence, and there is a brief stir between every person's attempt to make meaning of life and time. Death is certain; it may be the dust of good men and women lies more richly in the earth than that of the unjust; between the silences they may be touched, however briefly, with the music of the spheres.

GEORGE MACKAY BROWN, FOR THE ISLANDS I SING: AN AUTOBIOGRAPHY (1997)

Some build monuments, some carve their names on those monuments, some "make marks with a pen on paper": *all in the attempt to make meaning of their lives.* Our identities hold and collate that meaning. And maybe, as T. S. Eliot said, "home is where one starts from", but then he concluded, "old stones that cannot be deciphered" (both quotes are from "East Coker", from *Four Quartets* (1940)), or, maybe they can be? GMB's gravestone bears an inscription from the last two lines of his 1996 poem, "A Work for Poets":

> *Carve the runes*
> *Then be content with silence.*

Our silences may be touched with the music of the spheres or they may be lifted by Sir Peter Maxwell Davies' wonderful "Farewell to Stromness".

Carve the runes
Then be content with silence

GEORGE MACKAY BROWN

NICK ISBISTER

J. N. Isbister is an executive coach, and the author (with his wife, Jude Elliman) of The Story So Far: Introduction to Transformational Narrative Coaching, *The Isbister Press (2018).*

TO OBAN

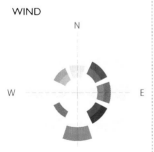

PASSAGE
Stromness to Oban

STOPS
Loch Clash ⚓
Summer Isles ⚓
Loch Ewe ⚓
Rona
Kyleakin
Arisaig
Small Isles ⚓ ⚓
Sound of Sleat ⚓
Mallaig
Tobermory
Kerrera ⚓

DISTANCE *(NM)*
393

PASSAGE TIME *(% +motor)*
70h (25%)

WIND

I F WE'D SEEN this on the south coast of England we would not have been surprised. But well off the north coast of Scotland we were astonished to pass a small open boat, with a single occupant, heading north-east. To the North Isles of Orkney? And then? Later Tom Cunliffe helped us identify it as most probably an Ian Oughtred design, a descendent of the Shetland Island Yoal. Perhaps it was going home.

We played "Farewell to Stromness" and sailed west, with our most experienced crew on board. In the event, the weather was kind; all day we watched the distant mountains and cliffs stretched out in sunshine and haze along the coast. As evening came, in a rising wind, we finally rounded the high cliffs of Cape Wrath at a respectful distance. The name comes not from its fearsome reputation but from the Old Norse *hvarf* ("turning point"). Surfing south in the evening sunshine, there was a great sense of satisfaction as we headed for shore and anchored in a small sheltered bay called Loch Clash, after a 13-hour passage.

The Shetland Yoal was one of several encounters with impressive sailors. We found different kinds in different places. In central London, the visiting yachts were Dutch. Further up the east coast, in May, we saw hardly any leisure boats at all – mainly we sailed alone. In Hull we saw only locals. In Edinburgh likewise. Then leaving Arbroath near Dundee we found ourselves in company with yacht *Shearwater*, also circumnavigating. Experienced and fearless, Jim and Angela sailed further and faster than we did, and got rather wetter as a result. We enjoyed their company on several occasions and compared notes.

By the time we reached Orkney, the boats were from Scandinavia and further afield, but still they were few and far between – we rounded Cape Wrath alone. Down the rugged north-west coast we continued to enjoy wide empty seas until we reached Skye. This felt like a long way south. Now it was July and holiday season, with sailors from all over the UK and Ireland. Suddenly things were getting crowded. Attempting to moor at Kyle Akin by the Skye Bridge, we were told there was officially no space, but we squeezed in alongside a glass-bottomed trip boat at the end of the pontoon, having been waved in enthusiastically by the de facto pontoon master. He was a sociable character living aboard his own boat nearby, who serenaded beautiful women on his boat late into the evening.

1. Heading for Shetland?
2. Cape Wrath
3. Kyle Akin
4. Acarsaid Mhor, Rona

1. *Nova* tacking hard up the Sound of Mull (image credit: *Cantata II*)

We had allowed extra time to enjoy these sheltered waters with friends. It was an overdose of scenery and stories in intriguing and romantic-sounding places like the Summer Isles, Rona (Acarsaid Mhor), Canna and Knoydart. There we spent a magical night moored in Doune Bay, dining on venison at one of the remotest restaurants in mainland Britain.

On 24 July we tied up at Kerrera Island in the shelter of Oban Bay. It's another place where coastal sailors mix with ocean adventurers, like Gary Hancock. Having retired as professional sailors, Gary and Kirstin have been voyaging in their yacht *Wandering Albatross*, campaigning for wildlife while sailing from the Arctic to Antarctic and now back in the North Atlantic. When we left to sail down the Scottish coast, they were about to set out for the Azores to pick up a dive team, head out into the Atlantic and anchor on an underwater "sea mount" to continue their work of marine conservation.

PILOT BOOKS
Clyde Cruising Club –
  Sailing Directions, Orkney and
  Shetland Islands incl. N and
  NE Scotland
Clyde Cruising Club –
  Sailing Directions,
  Ardnamurchan to
  Cape Wrath
Clyde Cruising Club –
  Sailing Directions, Kintyre to
  Ardnamurchan

ONLINE/APPS
www.visitmyharbour.com

▶ *McCaig's Tower overlooks the harbour at Oban*

THE LITTLE BAY WITH A BIG REPUTATION

MIKE ROBERTSON AND JOHN HOWE

TAKING ITS NAME from the Gaelic "An t-Òban" (The Little Bay), the influence of this west coast hub since the turn of the 19th century has been anything but small.

Oban has been a harbour since the earliest times; its famous bay is sheltered by the island of Kerrera, while Dunollie Castle sits atop a hill, guarding the entrance. We know that King Haakon of Norway gathered his fleet of galleys in the bay before the battle of Largs in 1263. However, the town and port of Oban started to become the hive of activity we know today in the 18th century, with a first custom house established in 1765, and the "official" distillery in 1794.

Over the next two centuries, the small town has developed at pace, thanks to its port, and has played a game-changing role in connecting the isolated Hebridean islands. It was a strategic outpost during World War II and has become a testing ground for new technologies.

Oban started to become the hive of activity we know today... with a first custom house... and the "official" distillery

This maritime heritage and ideal coastal location made Oban the perfect choice for the relocation of the marine research laboratory now known as the Scottish Association for Marine Science (SAMS) in 1969. Now one of this rural town's biggest employers, SAMS has helped to bring higher education to the area, as the research institute became a founding academic partner in the University of the Highlands and Islands. A fellow university partner, Argyll College, now also offers maritime skills courses from its Oban centre. Indeed, a conservative estimate of the student population of the town is 10 per cent of the resident 8,000 people.

By the 1850s, first David Hutcheson and then his son-in-law, David MacBrayne, established the regular ferry services

The rapid expansion of Oban began with the construction of the Crinan Canal in 1801, which made water transport from the Clyde to the port of Oban safer and more reliable. By the 1850s, first David Hutcheson and then his son-in-law, David MacBrayne, established the regular ferry services that revolutionised travel on the west coast. The ever-present and iconic black, white and red Caledonian MacBrayne ferries, as well as the pointed monument on the northern tip of Kerrera, the Hutcheson memorial, are a daily reminder of this feat.

Perhaps the biggest boost to Oban as a port came with the arrival of the railway, and the new railway pier in 1880. That meant that fish catches from Oban's then considerable fishing fleet could be unloaded straight onto trains and delivered to the city markets overnight. Fishing became a major industry for the harbour. Sadly, that has declined in recent years, but as late as the 1970s there would be a mass exodus of boats from the railway and south piers at one minute past midnight on a Monday morning. The sabbath had been observed.

During the autumn of 2013, SAMS deployed

There would be a mass exodus of fishing boats…
at one minute past midnight on a Monday morning.
The sabbath had been observed

state-of-the-art sonar technology to map the seabed in and around Oban Bay, an exercise that produced a surprising result. The bay was littered with the wreckage of flying boats, including Catalina, Short Sunderland and Saro Lerwick aircraft, damaged during World War II, when Oban was a base from which the Royal Air Force (RAF) Group Coastal Command defended the crucial North Atlantic convoys. Flying on such dangerous missions meant that pilots invariably had to negotiate landings on the water with parts of the aircraft badly damaged – another huge risk in itself.

Mapping the bay in this way meant charts more than 100 years old could be updated and the method has been used by SAMS elsewhere, as humans try to learn more about the deep ocean, an environment that remains alien to us and is less well explored than space. Divers and historians greeted the discovery of these wreckages in equal excitement, as Oban and the surrounding area was already regarded as a mecca for underwater enthusiasts.

Today Oban is a thriving port with, according to statistics, the largest number of daily ferry movements after Dover. It has always been a thriving hub for yachts and pleasure vessels, started by Queen Victoria visiting with the royal yacht in 1847 and continuing with annual events such as West Highland Yachting Week, when the boat owners from the Clyde race in company up to Oban and Tobermory for the start of their summer cruise. The new North Pier visitor pontoons established in 2017 have boosted the number of marine visitors using Oban as the starting place for charter boat voyages and provided improved facilities for visiting cruise liners.

The future management of the port is now under discussion with plans for a possible Trust Port arrangement to combine the interests of the community as a whole with those of the strictly commercial interests. The busy port is currently home to CalMac Ferries Ltd and Northern Lighthouse Board and Royal National Lifeboat Institution stations, amongst others.

Oban has been known as the "Gateway to the Isles", the seafood capital of the UK, a tourist town and now a university town and maritime hub. It is indeed a "little bay", but one with a sizeable reputation and significant continuing role in the development of the local area, and in the maritime story of the UK.

MIKE ROBERTSON

Originally from Edinburgh, Mike Robertson worked with Scottish Youth Hostels, helping with outdoor courses, including skiing, climbing and sailing. After graduating in law from the University of St Andrews in 1969, he was attracted by the sailing opportunities in Oban and moved to the town to work as a solicitor in 1971. He was one of the first crew members of Oban lifeboat when it was established in 1972 and served almost 30 years as crew. He is now the RNLI branch chairman.

JOHN HOWE

Senior lecturer in marine geology at the Scottish Association for Marine Science (SAMS), Dr John Howe is a keen diver. He is also programme leader for the SAMS Marine Science degree programme run through the University of the Highlands and Islands and leads the Graduate School on behalf of Scottish Alliance of Geosciences, Society and Environment (SAGES).

TO BELFAST

PASSAGE
Oban to Belfast

STOPS
Jura (Lussa Bay) ⚓
Gigha
Islay (Port Ellen)
Rathlin

DISTANCE *(NM)*
148

PASSAGE TIME *(% +motor)*
25h (68%)

WIND

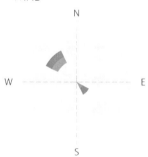

THE GLASGOW TRAIN came to a halt at Oban station and a bedraggled but cheerful family of four came chattering onto the concourse. Rain wasn't going to dampen their spirits, and that was just as well; our friends' first experience of yachting consisted of two dreich days seeing almost nothing.

After a night on board to acclimatise and our usual crew briefing, the next morning we set out in thick cloud, motoring past Seil and through the narrows at Fladda island. On down the Sounds of Luing and Jura, we regaled our novice crew with dramatic descriptions of the dangerous whirlpool at Corryvreckan, all invisible as we passed at a safe distance.

That night we dropped anchor at Lussa Bay on the island of Jura. For the first time, *Nova* felt like a small boat as we tackled the challenge of drying six people's wet-weather gear while conjuring up the illusion of civilised living. The rain stopped and several of us went ashore for a walk, greeted immediately by the sight of two impressive stags. Further on, we discovered the Lussa Gin distillery. As we were soon to learn, the Scottish islands have jumped on this trend with impressive enterprise. It is easier and quicker to make money from gin than from whisky.

4

Between us, Anne and I have family roots in England, Wales, Ireland and Scotland. My Scottish forebears manufactured gimlet-headed screws in Glasgow and I suspect they were teetotalling Presbyterians. Meanwhile Anne's great-grandfather, William Harvey, was busy testing water samples on the island of Islay before setting up a state-of-the-art distillery in 1881.

We sailed to Port Ellen and took a bus across to visit Bruichladdich Distillery. Anne was welcomed by private client manager Mary McGregor and discussed family archives. We toured the distillery, which today makes gin as well as whiskies, including Octomore, the smokiest (and costliest) I have ever tasted. Today the company is the largest private-sector employer on the island and despite various corporate takeovers (it is now owned by Rémy Cointreau) it maintains a distinctive community ethos. Island enterprise at its best, we thought.

5

1. Gigha island, en route from Jura to Islay

2. Whisky ageing in barrels at Bruichladdich

3. The original Victorian mash tun

4. East Light, Rathlin Island (with Mull of Kintyre visible)

5. Sampling Octomore Edition_09.2

Back at Port Ellen, the marina was crammed with Dutch yachts on a Round Britain Adventure Cruise. It was time to leave for Ireland. That involves crossing the North Channel, which is known for uncomfortable seas and strong tides. Our calculations were spot on; we arrived at the western point of Rathlin Island at slack water. But there was no slack we could find – the tide simply reversed and we fought 2 knots into the harbour at Church Bay.

Soon we were walking the cliffs where Marconi sent the first commercial radio transmission, looking east to Scotland and south down the Antrim coast, where we planned to continue to Belfast the next day. We could see fierce tides and rough water below us – the MacDonnell Race. It was named after the MacDonnell brothers, who were drowned there while returning to Rathlin. Their father, watching from land, raised his arm as if to move the boat's tiller to steer them out of harm's way. Legend has it that his arm stayed in the same position for the rest of his life.

PILOT BOOKS
Clyde Cruising Club –
    Sailing Directions,
    Kintyre to Ardnamurchan
Irish Cruising Club –
    East and North Coasts
    of Ireland, Sailing Directions
Welcome Anchorages 2019
    (publication) –
www.welcome-anchorages.co.uk

ONLINE/APPS
www.visitmyharbour.com
www.eOceanic.com

▶ *Titanic Belfast, from our mooring in Abercorn Basin*

TITANIC HARBOUR
ALF MCCREARY

THE HISTORY OF Belfast port is the story of the ingenuity and dogged determination of the local merchants, engineers and others who turned a mud-locked inlet into a world-class harbour, carving for itself a historic and unique niche in the maritime heritage of the British Isles.

The first-known sea chart of the area dates from 1570 and depicts the inlet as "Carrickfergus Lough", because of the trading pre-eminence of the town of Carrickfergus, a few miles north of Belfast.

However, by 1613, when Lord Chichester, on behalf of King James I, gave Belfast the status of a corporate borough, he permitted the establishment of a small port there, mainly to raise taxes for the Crown. Sadly, very little progress was made until the local merchants established a Ballast Board in 1785. There was little enough money available, but in 1791 William Ritchie arrived from Scotland with six jobbing carpenters to build wooden vessels, and eventually employed 118 workers.

The real breakthrough began when the Ballast Board members were given legal permission to begin cutting through the bends in the muddy inlet, which became known as Belfast Lough. The royal assent was granted by the newly crowned Queen Victoria in 1837, and money was raised to pay for the work.

A prominent Irish railway contractor, William Dargan, was appointed to make two cuts in the muddy channel, and by 1849 the access to the open sea was completed – just in time for Queen Victoria's one and only visit to Belfast.

During the long months of arduous work in forming the new channel, Dargan's workers dumped the mud (which he called "the stuff") into the mouth of the harbour to form "Dargan's Island". When the Queen came to Belfast, the grand new inlet was named, appropriately, Victoria Channel, and Dargan's Island became known as "Queen's Island". It was here that the impressive new iron ships were built, and given the dynamism of men like Sir Edward Harland and Gustav Wolff, the Harland and Wolff shipyard became one of the finest in the world.

One of the most significant developments of this period was the establishment in 1847 of the Belfast Harbour Board, most of whose members had served on the old Ballast Board. The new Harbour Board, whose members had the title of Harbour Board Commissioners, was responsible for running all aspects of the harbour and the estate, and generations of commissioners have continued in this role most successfully up to the present day.

Throughout the 19th century and well into the 20th, Harland and Wolff built a host of outstanding vessels. These included a range of transatlantic liners that took many of thousands of Irish emigrants to North America during that period of mass migration from Europe to the New World, and in return brought back large quantities of mail as a lucrative cargo. As the success of H&W grew, they added the outstanding entrepreneur William James Pirrie to the top management team.

The achievements of the Belfast shipyard were all the more remarkable because of the lack of local

The achievements of the Belfast shipyard were all the more remarkable because of the lack of local coal and steel

coal and steel in Ireland, both of which had to be imported from outside the island. Significantly, this gap in essential shipbuilding materials was overcome by the dedication of the Belfast workforce and their leaders.

By the end of the 19th century, Belfast was one of the greatest cities in the British Isles, and even more important than Dublin, to the latter's chagrin. The commercial success of the city was marked by the elegant extension to the Harbour Office in 1896 and also by the magnificent City Hall in 1906, both of which were completed by the local firm H&J Martin. Belfast was "no mean city" and the inhabitants were keen to underline this to the world at large.

Sadly, however, within two decades or so, everything had changed for the worse. The magnificent Olympic-class liners, the brainchild of William Pirrie and J. Bruce Ismay, Chairman of the White Star Line, to compete with Cunard, were launched in style in 1910 with the RMS *Olympic*, who sailed on her maiden voyage in June 1911. Tragically, however, her successor RMS *Titanic* made the wrong kind of maritime history when she hit an iceberg on her maiden voyage to New York in April 1912 and sank with the loss of over 1,500 lives.

The loss of the *Titanic* has never ceased to fascinate generations of people since then, but for nearly 100 years she was not talked about in Harland and Wolff or in Belfast generally. This was partly because people felt, illogically, that her sinking was the fault of the shipyard men who built her. It was treated like a death in the family.

Curiously it was only with the discovery of *Titanic*'s wreck, and the worldwide success of James Cameron's blockbuster movie, that Northern Irish people began to feel they could begin to talk openly about the vessel. There was even a hint of dark Belfast humour in the production of T-shirts for the increasing number of tourists who came to Belfast. The front of each T-shirt had a picture of the *Titanic*, and on the back was the legend "She was alright when she left us".

The Belfast shipyard Harland and Wolff and a smaller shipyard, Workman, Clark & Co., achieved significant production in the World War I era, but the intervening post-war years up until World War II were difficult for shipping and shipbuilding partly due to the worldwide depression. However, the Belfast Commissioners continued dredging, and completed a new airport and runway on the Harbour Estate just in time for the outbreak of World War II, during which the famous flying boats of Short & Harland Ltd also operated from Belfast. The harbour played a crucial role in keeping open the maritime lifeline with America, despite the horrendous Luftwaffe attacks on Belfast in 1941.

After World War II, Harland and Wolff continued

There was a hint of dark Belfast humour... "She was alright when she left us"

to build world-class vessels but their efforts were inevitably doomed to failure, despite generous government backing, because of stiff competition from world shipyards elsewhere. The economic realities of building great ships in Belfast was underlined by the launch in 1960 of *Canberra*, described as the "greatest British ship since the war", but its builders H&W lost £1.2 million on the contract. The company somehow has managed to survive and diversify, but at a greatly reduced level.

Meanwhile, throughout the decades of war and peace, the Belfast Harbour Commissioners have continued to maintain high levels of commitment and development within the Harbour Estate. This has been helped greatly in recent years by a huge influx of tourists and cruise liners, by the completion of the Titanic Centre on the site where the great ship was built, and by the growth of an impressive film industry: large parts of the iconic *Game of Thrones* and other major productions were filmed in the Belfast Harbour Estate and brought its name to a worldwide audience.

The harbour remains well-placed… to make the best advantage of the post-Brexit world

The harbour also remains well-placed technologically to make the best advantage of the entrepreneurial and other opportunities arising in the modern post-Brexit world, and the Harbour Board's Chief Executive, Joe O'Neill, announced recently their investment drive to create 10,500 jobs and to help boost Northern Ireland's economy. Mr O'Neill stated recently in the *Belfast Telegraph*, "There is the emergence of Belfast as an attractive city, and people are always looking at new markets."

The qualities of hard work, courage and ingenuity, which led to the establishment and development of Belfast Harbour from a muddy inlet in the 16th and 17th centuries to the world-class port it is today, are summarised by the distinguished Irish historian Dr Jonathan Bardon, who noted in his unsurpassed book *A History of Ulster*: "Many other ports in Ireland and Britain had similar problems to those of Belfast, but few had men as tenacious as members of the Harbour Board. Without their determination, Belfast might not have become one of the greatest ports in Western Europe, and certainly the city would not have become the home for a time of the largest shipyard in the world."

"Few (ports) had men as tenacious as members of Belfast's Harbour Board"

ALF MCCREARY
Alf McCreary is an award-winning Northern Ireland-based journalist, and author of a wide range of books including the bestselling Titanic Port: An Illustrated History of Belfast Harbour.

▶ *The cranes of Harland & Wolff, including Samson and Goliath*

TO DUBLIN

PASSAGE
Belfast to Dublin (Poolbeg)

STOPS
Bangor
Strangford
Carlingford

DISTANCE (NM)
155

PASSAGE TIME *(% +motor)*
27h (20%)

WIND

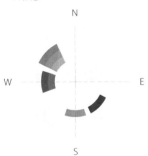

BELFAST WAS OUR decision point. Return north up the Antrim coast and then west round the whole of Ireland? Or play safe and sail south down the Irish Sea? That was our "plan B".

I love remote places, and the west coast was my dream. We had tasted the south-west corner once before: round Mizzen Head and across Bantry Bay in blazing sunshine accompanied by whales and gannets, to within sight of the mystical Skellig Islands. Could we go further and explore the whole west coast?

Navigationally we were well prepared. We had charts and guides, anchorages researched and waypoints marked. I had studied and imagined the shelter of Elly Bay in County Mayo and the white sands of Gurteen (Goirtín) in Galway. The boat and our equipment were up to the task, but were we? The west is exposed to everything the Atlantic can conjure.

I grew up with respect for the sea. Mainly that was from my grandfather, who taught me to sail in the days when navigation involved wobbly compass bearings and a cocked hat. Less talked-about in our family was the tragic death of my Irish great-uncle, many years ago. He was lost, so far as anyone knows, while returning to his boat by dinghy in the dark after dinner.

And so, aware of our own limits and the nature of the challenge, we had set ourselves two tests for this decision. We needed an experienced third crew member, confident to skipper if required. We also needed the weather to be settled. In the event, neither was forthcoming and on that basis the decision was made some time before we reached Belfast. We would head south.

Given the weather that followed, it was a good decision. On 8 August we left our mooring at the heart of Belfast's Titanic Quarter and headed for the popular harbour at Bangor, to replenish supplies and wait out some stormy weather before continuing down the coast. We were joined by Nigel, one of my Irish relatives, and we sailed through Donaghadee Sound towards Strangford Lough, a vast expanse of sheltered water, dotted with islets. It is said there's one for every day of the year.

Nigel guided us with softly spoken confidence through the 4-mile narrows, where unmarked shallows lurk and the stream runs at up to 8 kts. This ferocious tide sweeps through the moorings at Strangford itself, where we tied up on the pontoon near the ferry. We walked around the village in the evening sunshine and dined at the Lobster Pot. The gentleness of the scene belied its memories. We learned this was where my

1. We spent a night on the pontoon at Strangford (Photo: C.N. Eves)
2. Unloading the day's catch in Bangor harbour
3. *Nova* alongside former lightship *Petrel* at Ballydorn

great-uncle, Nigel's father, had dined before he was swept away.

Next morning, we sailed up the Lough, through Ringhaddy Sound and on to Ballydorn, where the Down Cruising Club has its headquarters in an old lightship. We'd heard about it from a club member we met in Scotland. "The tides run strong so just don't prang the commodore's boat," he had warned. We tied up alongside lightship *Petrel*. We seemed to be the only visitor. Once ashore, Nigel headed for home, and we walked across the fields to Daft Eddy's, a popular restaurant on nearby Sketrick Island, where we sampled steak and Guinness pie.

The following day we set out again. Accompanied by porpoises, we retraced our route out of the narrows and into an unexpectedly stiff south-easterly, which turned a 27-mile passage into a 40-mile beat to windward. By the end of the day we had crossed the border and were tied up beneath the Cooley Mountains in family-run Carlingford Marina, where they were experimenting with a "Universal Basic Berthage" rate for visiting yachts – you pay the same, whatever size your boat.

On 15 August, seizing our opportunity in offshore winds, we sailed south again: past Ireland's Eye, under the cliffs of the Ben of Howth, and into the shallows of Dublin Bay, passing a variety of impressive lighthouses. Once again we were heading for the heart of an impressive city. Guided by the watchful VTS (traffic controllers) we motored into the River Liffey along the Great South Wall and by nightfall we had squeezed into the only vacant space at Poolbeg Yacht Club, opposite cruise ships and container vessels in Ireland's largest and busiest port.

PILOT BOOKS
Irish Cruising Club –
    Sailing Directions, East and North
    Coasts of Ireland
Imray – Irish Sea Pilot

ONLINE/APPS
www.visitmyharbour.com
www.eOceanic.com

▶ *Samuel Beckett Bridge*

TAMING THE DANGEROUS BAY
LAR JOYE AND YVONNE SHIELDS O'CONNOR

LIKE MANY CAPITALS, Dublin has grown over the last 60 years, attracting people, business and government agencies. It is an international city with a large financial district based in the former docklands area, often referred to as "Silicon Docks" with almost 2 million people living in the metropolitan area. At the same time, Dublin Port has expanded and is now the largest port in Ireland.

Dublin was not always the country's dominant city. In the 17th century, Dublin Bay presented major dangers for shipping and trade with Britain and Europe. In 1674 its natural state was described as "wild, open and exposed to every wind, no place of shelter or security to ships". With strong tides, sandbanks and little shelter, ships frequently had to seek protection at two small seaside villages, Clontarf to the north or at Ringsend on the south of the city. In certain wind conditions ships could not reach the city for several weeks at a time. Shipwrecks were common, and it is estimated that at least fifteen hundred shipwrecks took place in the approach to Dublin Port. In addition the Liffey River silted up, denying ships access to the city, while many dumped excess ballast – needed when they were not full of cargo – into the river, causing blockages. As well as being dangerous to get to Dublin, too often on arrival it was impossible to enter.

It is estimated that at least fifteen hundred shipwrecks took place in the approach to Dublin Port

These were serious problems for an aspiring port. They were unlikely to be solved while port affairs were contested between Dublin Corporation and the Lord High Admiral in London, the then Prince Consort George. However, after the Corporation offered to pay the Prince annually 100 yards of Irish sailcloth, an act was passed entitled "An Act for Cleansing the Port, Harbour and River of Dublin and for Erecting a Ballast Office in the said City". The resulting Ballast Committee set to work and in 1716 began to build the South Bank and – when that proved ineffective – the South Bull Wall (bull is another word for strand).

After offering to pay the Prince annually 100 yards of Irish sailcloth an act was passed...

Over several decades the wall worked its way out to the Poolbeg Lighthouse and was finally completed in 1792. At the time it was the longest sea wall in the world, measuring 5 km.

Many Dublin merchants were dissatisfied at the slow progress of building the wall and in 1786 control of the port was transferred from Dublin Corporation to a new authority, the Corporation for Preserving and Improving the Port Of Dublin, which was controlled by merchants and property owners and also had responsibility for lighthouses in Dublin. Later in 1801 it was also given responsibility for maintaining lifeboats in Dublin Bay, and in 1810 under the Lighthouses (Ireland) Act, its lighthouse remit was extended to the whole island.

Even with the wall in place, almost a century later silting remained a problem. Greater ingenuity was required. In 1800 a major survey of Dublin Bay by Captain William Bligh (of HMS *Bounty* fame) recommended that a North Bull Wall be constructed to prevent sand building up in the mouth of the harbour. It was a controversial and clever plan. Bligh forecast that this new wall would hold back the water at high tide, diverting it to create a natural scouring action that would deepen the river channel where needed. It worked, and when the wall was completed in 1824 sand gradually accumulated along its side until an island emerged called Bull Island. Two hundred years later this is now a nature reserve, beach and part of the Dublin Bay UNESCO designated biosphere. Both walls are still providing the function of keeping the modern port open.

Throughout the 19th century the port expanded eastwards from the city, its growth fuelled by the arrival of the railway in 1840s, which made Dublin and the port the centre of a 4,200 km network

> *Captain William Bligh (of HMS Bounty fame)… forecast that this new wall would… create a natural scouring action that would deepen the river channel*

of railway track. This allowed travellers to leave the west of Ireland and be in London by the end of the day. A new custom house was built on reclaimed land, but the eastward shift for the city was opposed by many citizens who had their business in the older medieval city based around Dublin Castle.

From the 1860s construction work began on deep-water quay walls. More clever engineering was needed. Port Engineer Bindon Blood Stoney designed a 90-ton diving bell, crane and barge to speed up the building of the new quays. The bell was open at the bottom and allowed six workmen to descend down a funnel through an airlock to work on the riverbed. Their task was to level the riverbed to make way for large prefabricated concrete blocks, each weighing up to 350 tons. In 2014 Dublin Port Company decided to display the

> *A 4,200 km network of railway track allowed travellers to leave the west of Ireland and be in London by the end of the day*

diving bell, which had been saved, by raising it off the ground and building a small museum underneath. "Now suddenly, it's Dublin's newest museum – a miniature one, to be sure, but packing more fascination per square metre than most others" (Frank McNally, *Irish Times*). The museum has 110,000 visitors a year.

The Irish Free State was created… [and so] imports from England were no longer exempt from customs regulations

In 1867 came another name change, when the Dublin Port Act separated port activities into the newly constituted Dublin Port and Docks Board and the Lighthouse Department became the Commissioners of Irish Lights. A bespoke headquarters office was built for the port, with the Commissioners of Irish Lights next door demonstrating the close relationship that existed between the two organisations. What made the building famous and distinctive was the "Ballast Office Clock" mounted over the front door. In 1870 the clock was connected by telegraph wire to Greenwich Observatory, making this the most accurate public clock in Dublin at the time. It became established as a popular rendezvous point for people – "Meet you under the Ballast Office Clock" was a well-known refrain in Dublin.

The Irish Free State was created on 6 December 1922 with the last British Army soldier leaving on Sunday 17 December from Dublin Port. The consequences for the port were substantial as imports from England were no longer exempt from customs regulations. Bonded transit sheds, warehousing and customs facilities had to be built. During World War II Ireland remained neutral, a period that is called "The Emergency". Naturally fewer ships visited the port but expansion continued. The 1950s brought the first roll-on, roll-off services, and container traffic increasingly dominated port business from the 1960s.

Since 1997 the day-to-day running of Dublin Port has been managed by the Dublin Port Company (DPC), which traces its roots back 300 years. DPC is a self-financing private limited company wholly owned by the state. Previous tensions over the make-up of the board, labour strikes and the role of the government have been resolved as the port is now a landlord port with stevedoring and ferrying companies responsible for physically importing and exporting Irish trade.

Is this the end of the story? As Ireland's biggest port, Dublin continues to expand and the Dangerous Bay has been tamed through a combination of heavy engineering and aids to navigation. Irish Lights, while best known for its lighthouses, also operates a whole range of modern visual and electronic aids to navigation and maritime support services around the entire island of Ireland – protecting lives, property, trade and the environment around the coast. Since 1998, located in a new building across the bay in Dun Laoghaire, Irish Lights continues to collaborate with the port on important safety, navigation and heritage projects.

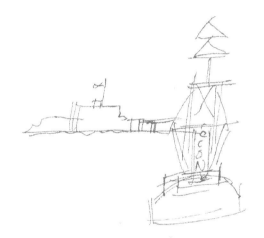

The port city of Dublin now looks to the future. Its ambition is set out in the DPC Masterplan (2012–40), which aims to improve the capacity of the port and reintegrate with Dublin city through its Port Perspectives Engagement Programme, protecting the nature reserves that surround it and reimagining the 300-year-old Port Archive, heritage infrastructure and buildings. This has supported a variety of artists, composers, actors and performers in the last four years including a very successful collaboration with the National Theatre in producing "In Our Veins" by Lee Coffey and "Last Orders at the Dockside" by Dermot Bolger. This embracing of theatre will continue in 2021 when award-winning theatre companies ANU Productions and Landmark Productions plan to stage a theatre show over six weeks to 8,000 people in the active port, based on its history.

Although affected by Brexit (and now the Coronavirus pandemic) the port city of Dublin, whose once dangerous bay was tamed through a story of ingenuity and politics, is now the economic jewel in Ireland's trading crown.

LAR JOYE

Lar Joye is Port Heritage Director at Dublin Port. A historian, curator and film archivist, he previously curated the award-winning Soldiers and Chiefs: The Irish Soldier at Home and Abroad from 1550 *exhibition at National of Museum of Ireland and played a key role in the Decade of Commemorations 2012–19, curating a number of exhibitions, conferences and theatre shows.*

YVONNE SHIELDS O'CONNOR

Yvonne Shields O'Connor is Chief Executive of Irish Lights. With a background in business and environmental science, she has worked for over 25 years in the marine and natural resource-based sectors in various roles in the public, not-for-profit and private sector, at national and international level.

TO HOLYHEAD

PASSAGE
Dublin (Poolbeg) to Holyhead

STOPS
Dun Laoghaire

DISTANCE *(NM)*
70

PASSAGE TIME *(% +motor)*
11h (23%)

WIND

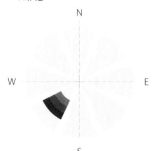

1

2

I N THE MUSEUM at the Mariners' Church in Dun Laoghaire there's a single faulty lightbulb on display. Scrawled on the glass is one word: *Titanic.* Apparently it was given by the son of an electrician, J. Nolan, who removed it in his checks before the great ship set out.

Almost every port we visited seemed to lay claim to the *Titanic* story. Belfast is where the liner is most prominently celebrated. However, Southampton arguably has the most personal links: of the 1,517 victims, more than 540 (all crew) came from that city. There were so many fathers and grandfathers that it is remembered there as a lost generation.

Shipwrecks are not the topic of choice when you're about to set out in a boat, but the coast is peppered with them. Those close to the surface are clearly marked on charts. It is sobering to see innumerable wrecks plotted on a map of Great Britain and Ireland.

It was 20 August when we found a weather window to depart from Dublin Bay. In a very gentle westerly breeze, we motored out from Dun Laoghaire into the Irish Sea. Passing the shipping lanes, we watched two ferries leaving Dublin, also heading east. Now we were on the historic route of the mail ships between Dublin and Holyhead.

The wind began to rise and moved around to the south-west, so we mounted the bowsprit and hoisted our huge Code Zero. Soon we were bowling along at 8 knots, heading slightly north to play the tide and ensure we would approach Holyhead from the north, well away from the strong currents around the Stacks.

Finally, after a long day's passage and with the rising wind raising an uncomfortable irregular sea, we rounded the breakwater and cautiously approached Holyhead marina. We were relieved to find there was space to tie up at the pontoon. It is the only one that remains after the marina was destroyed in 2018. Even the impressive Victorian breakwater wasn't enough to protect it from a freak storm coming from the north. Nearby, we found a hapless French solo sailor patching up his boat. On his arrival in the dark, he had collided with the unlit remains of one of the pontoons.

1. Leaving Dun Laoghaire harbour
2. Flying the Code Zero again
3. Moored next to former St David's lifeboat

We stayed put as strong southerly winds blew for several days. It gave us a chance to explore Anglesey and to spend a little time in Holyhead itself. In the nearby Maritime Museum I met Eric Anthony, a former boiler-maker for the ferries. His grandfather Robert had been a lamplighter on the beautiful and super-fast steamship RMS *Leinster*, which carried the mail to and from Dun Laoghaire. Sadly Robert died when the ship was torpedoed and sunk in World War I. I was horrified to learn that the loss of life was greater than the *Titanic*. They have no need to commemorate anyone else's shipwrecks here. They have more than enough of their own.

PILOT BOOKS
Imray – Irish Sea Pilot

ONLINE/APPS
www.visitmyharbour.com
www.eOceanic.com

▶ North Stack *twin-screw tug (1984) at Holyhead Marina*

GATEWAY TO IRELAND
IOLO GRIFFITHS

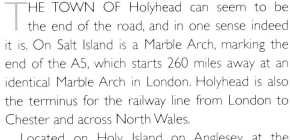

THE TOWN OF Holyhead can seem to be the end of the road, and in one sense indeed it is. On Salt Island is a Marble Arch, marking the end of the A5, which starts 260 miles away at an identical Marble Arch in London. Holyhead is also the terminus for the railway line from London to Chester and across North Wales.

Located on Holy Island on Anglesey, at the western tip of North Wales, historically the port of Holyhead has been an important staging post and mail route to Ireland. Nowadays it is a vital link on the European road haulage network, with transcontinental lorries and holidaymakers on their way across the Irish Sea. They embark efficiently from road or rail without needing to visit the town itself, which can seem somewhat down-at-heel, especially if you go there on a Sunday and find hardly anything is open.

The Romans [used] a watchtower on Holyhead Mountain to keep surveillance for Irish pirates

In recent years this busy port has also become a stop for cruise ships, though it can be expected that the bulk of the cruise visitors see very little of Holyhead, as they take excursions to more glamorous destinations such as Snowdonia or one of the several castles for which Wales is famed.

However, despite often being overlooked, Holyhead offers a vast number of places of interest for people with an open mind, and particularly for maritime history enthusiasts. The Maritime Museum on Newry Beach (a name that echoes links with the Emerald Isle), housed in a former lifeboat house, is an obvious place to start on exploring the town's maritime history, and the town's marina is nearby.

The port's role in trade with Ireland may in fact go as far back as 2000 BC, when stone axes from Ireland were the main import. The area surrounding the town certainly has many megalithic sites, showing the area's importance in that era.

In Roman times the locality's strategic position was utilised by the Romans, with a watchtower on Holyhead Mountain to keep surveillance for Irish pirates. In the town itself is a fortification overlooking the harbour, which served as a Roman coastguard station. In the sixth century Prince Caswallon, prince of North Wales, gave this fortification to Saint Cybi, the town's patron, who built his church within the walls.

Holyhead's strategic position meant that in the Middle Ages it sometimes played a role as an embarkation point for invasions of Ireland. In July 1332 orders were given for ships from Gloucestershire, Devon, Cornwall, North and South Wales to assemble at Holyhead and Tenby for a projected invasion to be led by Edward III, but due to the threat from Scotland this came to nothing.

In Tudor times royal dispatches from London passed through Holyhead on the way to the officials in Dublin, and initially this service was restricted to official communications, but later on, private correspondence was also carried.

In the days before reliable steam ferries, sailings relied on favourable weather, and passengers were sometimes forced to spend days in lodgings in the

town. One of these unwilling guests in 1727 was Dean Jonathan Swift, the author of *Gulliver's Travels*, who dined on good mutton, but the worst ale in the world, and complained that none of the local farmers and shopkeepers spoke English. In 1748 John Wesley was similarly forced to tarry in Holyhead, because the ships were all on the other side of the Irish Sea, but at least he put this time to good use by preaching the gospel.

Jonathan Swift, the author of Gulliver's Travels... *dined on good mutton, but the worst ale in the world*

After the Act of Union with Ireland in 1801, Irish MPs started travelling to Westminster, which led to the need to improve the road connecting London to Holyhead and Ireland, and subsequently to the building of the famed Menai Suspension Bridge, an object of beauty and a marvel of engineering, and later the construction of the railway line and the Britannia Bridge, also relating to connecting Dublin to the capital.

From Newry Beach you can see a breakwater, which is just under two miles long, snaking away into the distance. The work on this vast project started in 1848 and finished in 1873, with a lighthouse at the end. It had become clear that a harbour of refuge was needed to shelter ships from south-westerly gales (in 1826 it had been reported that over 150 ships sought shelter at Holyhead). Brunel's *Great Eastern*, then the biggest ship in the world,

sheltered behind the unfinished breakwater 25–26 October 1859, the night of the storm that was to become famous for the sinking of the *Royal Charter*, at the opposite end of Anglesey.

Seven million tonnes of stone were quarried from Holyhead Mountain for building this breakwater, extracted from a quarry at the other end of Newry Beach and transported on temporary railway lines. This is now a quiet beauty spot, with a lake, rocky coast, walks and some relics of the industrial past. Reclaimed by nature, in 1990 it was opened as the Holyhead Breakwater Quarry Park.

Brunel's Great Eastern, *then the biggest ship in the world, sheltered behind the unfinished breakwater*

The work involved in building the breakwater resulted in an influx of people taking advantage of the labour opportunities presented. This resulted in a phenomenal increase in population, from 3,809 in 1841 to 8,863 in 1851, with a swarm of navvies and workmen, and also better-off classes such as civil engineers, naval commanders and ships' officers, and an influx of English and Irish into the town.

The town's dependence on trade with Ireland is a strong point when relations with the neighbouring island are good, but this was emphatically not the case in the 1930s, with a trade war between the UK and the Irish Free State. Unemployment was high in Holyhead at the time, though the town's wartime role as a naval base for the Dutch navy helped to alleviate this.

Ferries to Ireland still keep the port buzzing with

Ferries to Ireland still keep the port buzzing

people and activity, but they're not the only vessels bound for Ireland. Today there are more than 500 calls per year from bulk carriers, cruise ships, coasters and large fishing vessels, plus numerous smaller fishing vessels and leisure craft.

Over the years, the port has enabled diverse industries to thrive. You may be able to see a very tall chimney to the east of the town. This chimney, visible on a clear day from almost the centre of Anglesey, is a reminder of what was once the town's major employer.

Anglesey Aluminium, a joint venture of Rio Tinto Zinc and Kaiser Aluminium, started producing in 1971. Several factors made Holyhead an ideal location: being a port made it accessible for raw materials, while the road and railway links would help in transporting the finished material. It also had access to the vital resources of electricity from the Wylfa nuclear power station, water from the Llyn Alaw reservoir and labour from the town. Sadly the contract for power from Wylfa terminated in 2009, and no new contract was negotiated, so the main aluminium plant closed. Much of the site is now occupied by the Penrhos Retail Park, which does create substantial employment for the area, but diverts passing traffic from the town centre.

As heavy industry has declined, Holyhead has looked for renewal. Tourism could be boosted by an eco-park including business units and a holiday village on former industrial land. Ambitious plans for biomass power generation have had hopes raised.

Plastics reprocessing gives a boost to Holyhead's green credentials. Novel forms of tidal power generation are being trialled offshore. The port is planning for all Brexit scenarios. The marina, destroyed by a freak storm in 2018, plans to rebuild.

Holyhead may be at the end of the road, and its resilience has been tested, but it's not the end of the road for Holyhead.

As heavy industry has declined, Holyhead has looked for renewal... Ambitious plans for biomass power generation have had hopes raised

IOLO GRIFFITHS

Iolo Griffiths is a community content curator with the Daily Post *and associated weekly newspapers in North Wales. He is a native of Anglesey and is keenly interested in genealogy and the history of North Wales. He has written a number of books on local history, including:* A History of Beaumaris; History of Bangor; A History of Holyhead; History of Amlwch; History of Conwy; History of Caernarfon; *and* Crossing the Menai Strait, *which traces the history of the ferries and bridges across the Menai Strait.* Maritime Dynasty: History of the Griffiths Family *traces a century of maritime history from the viewpoint of three generations of Nefyn sailors, with strong links to Liverpool, the capital of North Wales.*

▶ *For several days Nova sheltered behind the breakwater at Holyhead*

TO MILFORD HAVEN

PASSAGE
Holyhead to Milford Haven

STOPS
Brief stop at Porth Dinllaen

DISTANCE *(NM)*
145

PASSAGE TIME *(% +motor)*
27h (59%)

WIND

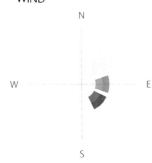

THE WIND THREATENED to blow us off our feet as we looked down from the cliffs on Holy Island. Two kestrels hovered miraculously in the gusts, falling to stay still. Below us was a small pedestrian bridge crossing a chasm to South Stack Lighthouse, and beneath it, the water boiled. It was one of those days we were glad to be on land.

Offshore we could see the wild seas that accompany wind-against-tide conditions off the Anglesey coast. This is the why lighthouses exist. This one was built in 1809 to warn ships en route between Dublin, Holyhead and Liverpool.

Three days later the wind had abated and we cast off soon after dawn on 24 August. A quick radio call to the harbour cleared us to round the end of Holyhead Breakwater and head south, sailing close inshore where the water was now calm. Out to sea we could just see the buoys marking the world's first low-flow tidal stream energy project in Holyhead Deep.

Sailing gently towards the Llyn peninsula, we planned to break our journey overnight at Porth Dinllaen, having spent the past day or so attempting to pronounce it. Arriving at the anchorage, we found British holidaying at its noisiest best. The sandy beach was full of sunbathers while speedboats and jet-skis buzzed about, dragging screaming children in rubber rings. We'd hoped for the Ty Coch Inn for dinner but discovered it closes early.

That tipped it – we advanced our plan by 12 hours and set out again into the warm gentle evening, leaving the happy chaos behind.

Night fell as we approached Bardsey Island, a historic place of pilgrimage known as the "island of 20,000 saints". As we sailed past we could see the red and white stripes of the tallest square-towered lighthouse in the UK. Built in 1821, these days it is solar powered, and LEDs flash red. It was one of the more unusual we saw on our voyage, along with the West Light on Rathlin Island (also red, and upside down), the disused lightships at Harwich, and the Great Light on display in Belfast, with its 10-tonne Fresnel hyper-radial lenses.

We switched on our navigation lights and continued into the night, for only the second time in the voyage. Like our east-coast night passage across the Wash, here in Cardigan Bay there are few if any places for a deep-draft yacht to call in, and a straight line south makes sense. The wind died and we motored on, steered by the autohelm.

Night still holds some fear for me, but it can be magical on a clear calm night with stars above, the hypnotic sound of the sea and the reassuring sight of lighthouses in the distance. Sometimes the sea lights up with phosphorescence. The sensation of speed is extraordinary too – you could be hurtling along at ten times the actual speed. It's impossible to tell.

After a while, however, especially in the early hours, the magic gives way to tedium. In this case the tide turned and our progress slowed. There was no passing traffic. Strumble Head Lighthouse seemed to be on our port bow forever as we kept watch in pairs, doing two-hour shifts in rotation. Eventually

1. South Stack lighthouse
2. Sailing along the Lleyn peninsula
3. The Ty Coch Inn
4. We sailed through the night across Cardigan Bay

PILOT BOOKS
Imray – Irish Sea Pilot

ONLINE/APPS
www.visitmyharbour.com
www.eOceanic.com

Strumble was behind us, and in the dawn light Anne and Alan on watch reported seeing dolphins playing around the boat. I checked our position on the chart plotter and came on deck. In front of us, to starboard in the distance was another lighthouse at The Smalls, and closer to hand was South Bishop Light. It is hard to imagine how anyone could build a structure like that, on top of a steep-sided rock off the wild tidal Atlantic coast, but in 1839 somehow they did. Until the age of GPS, vessels relied on them to triangulate their position at night. Even today they provide an unerring visual check, and they gave us reassurance as we passed the Bishops and Clerks (rocks), headed for the gap between Skomer and Skockholm (islands), rounded the battery at St Anne's Head, and entered the familiar, broad and sheltered waters of Milford Haven.

▶ *Stack Rock Fort (1859)*

MILFORD HAVEN
51° 42' 42'' N, 5° 02' 24'' W

83

DREAMS AND VISIONS
SIMON HANCOCK

MILFORD HAVEN IS one of the world's great deep-water harbours, a ria formed by the submergence of a river valley that extends inland some 30 kilometres before rising into the Eastern and Western Cleddau rivers. The Welsh name for the harbour is Aberdaugleddau or "mouth of the two rivers Cleddau". The upper reaches are predominantly farmland and woods while the lower ria, near the mouth of the Haven, is industrial and urban in character with energy industries and larger towns of Milford Haven, Pembroke Dock and Neyland.

The advantages of Milford Haven were recognised in antiquity during the Roman colonisation and Viking raids in the ninth and tenth centuries. The Haven grew in importance following the arrival of the Normans from 1093 and arrival of thousands of Flemish migrants during the early years of the 11th century. On account of Pembrokeshire's strategic location as an important staging post for Ireland, the harbour witnessed the departure of several English kings including Henry II, John and Richard II as they embarked on campaigns. In the Middle Ages ships traded to Ireland, Bristol and continental Europe exporting wool, coal, leather and agricultural produce from prosperous borough ports that existed at Pembroke and further upriver at Haverfordwest.

On 7 August 1485 Henry Tudor arrived from France and landed on the Dale peninsula, near the mouth of the waterway, en route to victory at Bosworth Field, which secured him the crown of England. William Shakespeare referred to Milford in two of his plays, *Richard III* and *Cymbeline*. In Act III of the latter he gave Imogen the memorable line:

Tell me how Wales was made so happy as T'inherit such a haven.

In 1753 a Bristol merchant built a large warehouse at Barnlake near Neyland to import West Indian goods, especially sugar. Both sides of the haven had various quays and communities where small-scale shipbuilding was carried out. As a port in its own right, the town of Milford Haven can be dated back to 9 June 1790 when local landowner Sir William Hamilton (1730–1803) obtained an Act of Parliament to create a new town – taking its name from the haven – to "provide quays, docks and piers". In 1792 some 23 Quaker families including the Starbucks and Folgers were encouraged to settle the new community from their home on Nantucket Island in the United States, with the goal of establishing a whaling fleet. The Royal Navy Board also agreed to establish a new naval dockyard at the mouth of Hubberston Pill in 1796, although this lasted a little more than a decade.

Hamilton scored a spectacular publicity coup for his new town when he secured the visit of Vice Admiral Horatio Nelson in 1802. The great hero declared the harbour of Milford Haven to be the best harbour in the world after Trincomalee in Ceylon. Capitalising on its moment of fame, the New Inn at which the party dined was later renamed the Lord Nelson Hotel in his honour.

The port of Milford Haven grew with a post office packet station sailing to Ireland, and as the town grew plans were developed to build spacious docks. An Act of Parliament was secured for that purpose in 1874 but a series of engineering difficulties and contractor bankruptcies led the project taking 14 years to complete rather than the anticipated three years. During the work on the docks, Brunel's last and most ill-fated ship, the *Great Eastern*, was berthed at Milford Haven from 1875 to 1886, laid up and with no purpose until she weighed anchor to steam to Liverpool to be used as an exhibition ship. It had been intended to attract transatlantic passenger ships to call into the haven and despite the well-publicised arrival of the *City of Rome* (1889) with 134 passengers, such transatlantic visitors were few and far between.

The docks were finally completed in 1888 and the first vessel to enter was not a transatlantic passenger liner as the Docks Company had long hoped but the 127-ton trawler *Sybil*. This turned out to be the start of Milford Haven's famous association with an industry that drove economic expansion, rising population and the development of public services. By 1901 the town's population stood at 5,102. The fishing industry enjoyed astonishing growth well into the 20th century so that the number of fishing vessels entering the docks rose from 12 to 323 during the period 1889–1908. The tonnage of fish landed rose from 9,500 tons in 1890 to 44,283 in 1913. Around 4,000 people were employed by the fishing industry and there were 100 fish buyers living locally in the early 1920s. The industry had a dedicated railway spur, ice factory, box factory and numerous ancillary services required for Wales's largest fishing port and the fifth largest in the United Kingdom. Two world wars clearly impacted on the industry as trawlers were taken for national defence, although access to under-fished stocks at the end of both wars saw bumper years follow. The record catch was witnessed in 1946 with 59,000 tons but from then on there was a slow but inexorable decline. By 1970 only 4,000 tons of fish was landed, and the number of trawlers was down to single figures by the late 1980s.

By then the focus of the port had long shifted to an industry that could take full advantage of the haven's deep water and undeveloped land: oil. The first refinery was constructed by Esso at a cost of £18 million in 1960. Over the following decade other oil companies expended huge sums to build a further three refineries. Around the same time a 2000 MW oil-fired power station was built near Pembroke and was operational 1968–2000 before it was demolished, and a second gas-fired power station opened on the same site on 19 September 2012. Between 1983 and 2014 three of the refineries closed due to international competition, overcapacity and cost pressures. The remaining oil refinery, now owned by Valero, continues to play a vital role in the Pembrokeshire economy, and Milford Haven's role as a leading energy port continues with liquified natural gas (LNG) terminals replacing oil. These supply almost a third of the country's gas requirements.

The age of oil came with a human and environmental cost. In particular, local people remember the tragic incident of 2 June 2011 when four refinery workers at Valero died in an explosion. The grounding of the *Sea Empress* tanker on 15 February 1996 resulted in 73,000 tons of crude oil being spilled, devastating some of the country's most important maritime habitats. There has since been a remarkable recovery, but the beauty of Pembrokeshire's landscape still sits uneasily alongside the industry that sustains its economy.

> *The age of oil came with a human and environmental cost*

Today this place continues to follow the ebb and flow of prosperity, decline and reinvention. The statutory harbour authority is an independent non-profit Trust Port, which developed from the original Milford Haven Conservancy Act (1958). Transportation is at the core of operations and includes the safe navigation, cargo handling and ferry services to Ireland from Pembroke Dock. As well as LNG traffic the port still has the largest fishing docks in Wales, while leisure and tourism are vital sectors to the prosperity of the port. Leisure marinas operate at Neyland and Milford, and cruise ships are encouraged. Nine ships called in during the year 2017–18, bringing in 4,100 passengers. Perhaps the dreams of ocean liners at Milford Haven are finally being fulfilled.

SIMON HANCOCK

Dr Simon Hancock was born in Neyland and his family has a long-standing association with the Milford Haven waterway. An author and keen local historian by interest and by profession, he is curator of Haverfordwest Museum, chair of the Pembrokeshire Historical Society and in 2015 obtained a PhD from Cardiff University for his thesis on Pembrokeshire in World War I. Simon is involved in local charities, including Torch Theatre and Neyland Heritage. He has held many other public offices including serving on Neyland Town Council since 1987, as a magistrate, and as chairman of Pembrokeshire County Council 2019–20.

▶ Milford Haven seeks to combine industry with tourism

TO BRISTOL

PASSAGE
Milford Haven to Bristol

STOPS
Dale ⚓
Tenby
Oxwich Bay ⚓
Cardiff

DISTANCE *(NM)*
125

PASSAGE TIME *(% +motor)*
20h (11%)

WIND

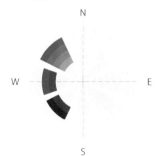

"WHEN EXACTLY WILL you arrive?" It's a question that made us smile, given the variables of British weather and tides. We tried not to promise any of our crew exactly where we would be, and when. But people need to make a plan.

Rashly before our departure we had therefore circulated a detailed itinerary of our entire voyage, with dates and locations getting gradually more vague. Relying on this, my cousin from New Zealand had booked her flights to join us in Milford, together with Dai, a friend whose Welsh roots drew him back. They both needed to leave us in Bristol a few days later. Now we had to deliver.

It's hard to explain to non-sailors how long it takes to prepare a single day's sailing. Most days Anne, as chief navigator, spent up to two hours of passage planning and research the old-fashioned way with tide tables and pilot books. For the Irish Sea and St George's Channel, that included my grandfather's 1962 tidal stream atlas; the moon, after all, hasn't shifted much in half a century. Then we went through the plan together and I cross-checked with tidal information on an iPad, double and triple-checking the timings and guidance for each port and discussing back-up plans. Finally I entered waypoints on the iPad and transferred them to the plotter. It was exhausting, especially at the end of a long day's sailing.

1. Savvy Navvy charts a course for Cardiff

2. My grandfather's tidal stream atlas

3. A brief stop on the pontoon at Dale

If we had consulted the tidal atlas for the Bristol Channel months before, we would have discovered the flaw in our published itinerary. In our chosen week, eastbound tides were getting late in the day. As we looked closely at the tide tables we realised if we were to set out even one day later than planned, we'd be arriving in the dark at an unfamiliar port or anchorage. Luckily for us, right on cue the weather eased and we departed from Milford in the early evening of 31 August, sailing to Dale in the remains of the strong south-westerly breeze. As we anchored for the night, the chain rattled on and on until we'd let out enough scope to allow for the 10-metre tidal range.

Next day we set out against the tide, catching a favourable eddy in Freshwater West through the firing range (closed at weekends). We rolled and bounced slowly around St Govan's Head and then as the tide turned we broad-reached in sunshine at speed past the bays and beaches of Pembrokeshire's stunning coastline. Through Caldey Sound, Tenby's pastel-coloured seafront came into view. On local advice, we picked up a substantial mooring in time to go ashore and sample some local delicacies.

The next two days were more challenging. We had picked Oxwich Bay as our staging post en route to Cardiff, looking for hops that could be achieved in a single east-going tide (six hours). Triple-checking our options, I turned to my latest app, called Savvy Navvy. It is made for this kind of puzzle, combining wind and tidal predictions to propose a route with clever algorithms that compress hours of planning into seconds. The results are best used with judgement, to check other calculations, and the early versions of the

3

app had some odd quirks, but it is a hugely valuable secondary aid.

We've learned the importance of local human advice too, and after a phone call to the local RNLI station for advice on rounding Worm's Head ("go outside the cardinal mark, not through Helwick Swatch") we set out at 2 p.m. It was a fast passage in F5–6 but I wished for less south in it. Rounding the point into Oxwich there was nobody else at anchor and I was afraid the swell, which typically curves around corners, would find its way right into the anchorage. If it was untenable, there would be no alternative but to continue into the night. Fortunately the anchorage was calm, if rather brief. Four different alarm ringtones woke us at 3:30 a.m. and we set out in the dark at 4:00 a.m. Racing past the lights of Port Talbot at almost 10 kts (ground speed), we were in Cardiff Bay by 9:30 a.m.

From Cardiff the short final leg to Bristol was uneventful and swift. Again we were travelling at 10 kts (aided by 4 kts tide) and as we approached the River Avon and sailed gently up the gorge, we began to feel the weight of global maritime history in this place. Like sailors for 150 years, we turned our gaze from the brown mud-laden river beneath us to Brunel's Suspension Bridge and the blue sky beyond. On through the sea lock and we had arrived – shipshape and Bristol fashion.

PILOT BOOKS
Bristol Channel Yachting
  Association – The Blue Book
  (Yachting and Cruising Guide
  to the Bristol Channel)

ONLINE/APPS
www.visitmyharbour.com
www.eOceanic.com

TIDAL INFORMATION
Printed Tide Tables
  (with Almanac)
Navionics
Imray Tides Planner app
Savvy Navvy

▶ *Dockside crane (1951)*

SHIPSHAPE AND BRISTOL FASHION

TIM BRYAN

YOU CAN'T SEE the sea from Bristol Docks – it's eight miles down the River Avon at Avonmouth, where the city's modern dock facilities are. These grew steadily from the 1870s onwards when the original harbour in the centre of the city became too small to cope with the growth of trade and the bigger ships that went with that.

As early as 1051 the Anglo-Saxon Chronicle recorded that Bristol was trading with Ireland, and by the 16th century it was already a major maritime centre with ships sailing upriver to a harbour built at the confluence of rivers Avon and Frome. The cargoes unloaded on the dock came from other British ports and more distant locations in Europe and beyond. A few years earlier in 1497, the explorer John Cabot had set out on the transatlantic voyage that would ultimately lead to him discovering the coast of North America and landing there very briefly.

In 1497, the explorer John Cabot set out [from Bristol] on the transatlantic voyage that would ultimately lead to him discovering the coast of North America

The tobacco, sugar and cocoa that flowed into the city docks in the 17th and 18th centuries enabled Bristol to grow and become rich, reflected in the streets of elegant Regency houses built in the centre and up the hill in Clifton. Fuelling that prosperity was industry, created to process raw materials brought across the Atlantic from the West Indies. All this was at a human cost: for 15 years between 1730 and 1745, Bristol was Britain's most important port in the slave trade and the shadow of slavery continues to fall across communities in the city long after its abolition.

The shadow of slavery continues to fall across communities in the city

Maritime connections are hard to avoid in the city; Bristol is thought to be the birthplace of Edward Teach, better known as Blackbeard, the infamous and brutal pirate. Alexander Selkirk, the inspiration for Robert Louis Stevenson's Robinson Crusoe, was rescued by a Bristol ship and brought back to the city, where he met the author in the famous Bristol pub The Llandoger Trow.

Busy as Bristol was, trade was hampered by the fact that the harbour was tidal. This might not sound important, but the difference between low and high tide in the docks and river could be up to 40 feet (the Bristol Channel still has the second highest range in the world). This made operating a dock very difficult as ships were left high and dry when the tide went out. Mariners had to be prepared, "shipshape and Bristol fashion".

The solution was to build what is now called the Floating Harbour, an area of tideless water enclosed by dock gates. Designed by William Jessop and opened in 1809, the new harbour improved matters and also led to a further flowering of Bristol's shipbuilding industry.

Into this picture strode the Victorian engineering giant Isambard Kingdom Brunel. Brunel arrived in Bristol in 1829 having survived a near-fatal accident in the Thames Tunnel the year before. Soon he was

SS Great Britain

involved in various engineering projects, winning a competition to design a new suspension bridge at Clifton in 1831 and working for the Dock Company, providing designs for ways of preventing the harbour from silting up. In 1833 he was then appointed as the engineer of the Great Western Railway, a new scheme to build a line from Bristol to London.

If all that was not enough, the lure of the sea provided too much for even Brunel. There is an apocryphal if fanciful story that in a discussion about the speed at which passengers could be whisked from London to Bristol on his new railway, he asked, why not extend the journey by linking Bristol and New York with a steamship? Whatever was actually said or decided, the end result was the creation of the Great Western Steamship Company, financed by local business interests, and the construction of the SS *Great Western* in 1838, a wooden paddle steamer that began the process of making transatlantic travel a quicker and safer prospect.

Following the ship's 15-day maiden voyage to New York in April 1838, it began a regular service between Britain and the United States. Most observers then thought that the company would repeat the exercise and built a sister ship, but Brunel, restless as ever, had moved on, and instead proposed a new, bigger steamship that had

> *"Why not extend the railway journey from London by linking Bristol and New York with a steamship?"*

revolutionary new features. Not only it would be made of iron, but it would have a screw propeller; when the SS *Great Britain* was launched in 1843, it was the largest ship in the world and was described as the "wonder of the age".

It began by first speeding travellers across the Atlantic, and from 1852 it carried thousands of emigrants to Australia for over 20 years. After a further brief life as a windjammer (under sail alone) it was shipwrecked in the Falkland Islands in 1886, and remained there until 1970, when it was rescued and brought back to the UK. The SS *Great Britain* was brought back to the dockyard where it had been built over a century before and to a harbour much changed since its launch. The construction of new docks at Avonmouth in the Victorian period and their subsequent expansion in the 20th century had hastened the demise of the city docks, now too small to handle larger ships and hampered by the difficult river journey up the Avon from the Bristol Channel.

> SS Great Britain *was shipwrecked in the Falkland Islands in 1886, and remained there until 1970*

By the time the SS *Great Britain* returned in 1970 the Floating Harbour was in terminal decline, with both dock facilities and shipbuilding very reduced – just a few years earlier, proposals to build a new road system and fill in parts of the docks had been made, and then abandoned after protests from Bristolians. We at the SS *Great Britain* can't claim that we were responsible for the amazing transformation that has taken place since 1970, but as we celebrate the 50th anniversary of the ship's return in 2020, we can argue that we perhaps provided the spark. The regeneration of the city docks has provided treasured cultural centres such as the Arnolfini, Watershed and M Shed Museum, as well as housing and leisure facilities.

Bristol remains a vibrant city, its development now powered and sustained by its multicultural community, new technology and industry, universities, and arts and cultural life. The docks remain at the heart of the city, now reclaimed by local people and tourists, with huge swathes of what was a bustling port 100 years ago accessible to all and providing some recognition of how much the city owes to its long and rich maritime past.

> *The regeneration of the city docks has provided new cultural treasures…*

Tim Bryan

Tim Bryan is Director of the Brunel Institute at the SS Great Britain Trust (www.ssgreatbritain.org) and a trustee of the RNLI Heritage Trust. He is moved by things that move: his previous roles included Head of Collections at the British Motor Museum in Warwickshire and Manager at STEAM, the Museum of the GWR in Swindon. Tim was awarded the Fellowship of the Museums Association in 2016 and for 10 years he has chaired the Association of British Transport & Engineering Museums, a heritage network that published Guidelines for the Care of Larger and Working Historic Objects in 2018. He lives in Swindon and has written 20 books on railway and heritage subjects, including a biography of Brunel; his most recent, Railway Carriages, was published by Shire in 2019.

▶ *Passing SS Great Britain in Bristol's Floating Harbour*

LEG **11** TO FALMOUTH

PASSAGE
Bristol to Falmouth

STOPS
Cardiff
Lundy ⚓
Padstow
Newlyn

DISTANCE *(NM)*
249

PASSAGE TIME *(% +motor)*
40h (12%)

WIND

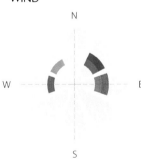

BRISTOL IS OFF the beaten track for cruising yachts, so there were relatively few visitors, and the facilities were spartan. However, once again to my delight we had tied up in the very heart of a major city: one that has an intoxicating blend of maritime history and present-day culture.

Music had naturally been a rich part of our journey so far. In Bristol we stepped ashore to find talented local bands playing in the streets and in clubs, and even a hilarious silent disco on the dockside one night. We remembered all the other places we had sampled local music: a formal military band in Stromness; Scottish musicians playing around a table laden with drinks in the Crofters Bar at Arisaig; a talented duo in a Belfast pub; and a loud, wild Welsh band letting loose in Holyhead.

On 13 September, on schedule and with fresh crew, we set out again down the Avon, past the commercial port, and into the soupy-brown sea. The passage out of Bristol might, I feared, be more difficult than any other part of our journey. Why? First, it's against the prevailing wind. Second, as before, it is essential to go with the tide. But this time, heading out, you'll arrive at your destination at low tide. That cuts down the options for daytime passages almost to nil.

Smiled on again by fair winds and sunshine, we retraced our steps to Cardiff for a night, before locking out early, rounding Lavernock Point and heading west. Our goal was Lundy Island, where we hoped to

anchor in Landing Bay. Today's "plan B" was to carry on overnight to Padstow on the north Cornish coast, where we would need to anchor and wait for the tide in the morning.

As we progressed towards the island, muddy water gave way to turquoise. If you'd been watching from the high cliffs you would have seen us approach, slowly circle the bay and find a spot to drop the hook securely in the sand. Once anchored we pumped up the dinghy, lowered the electric outboard and purred our way quietly to the shore, where we were greeted by a curious young seal. There was an even younger pup on the beach nearby – white and fluffy, just two weeks old – with its Atlantic Grey mother and dominant male standing guard in the water.

After a stroll across the island to ascend the lighthouse, we dined at the Marisco Tavern (open 24/7), and as dusk fell retraced our steps back down the cliff path to our dinghy and back to *Nova*, whose anchor light we had left on in readiness. As we settled for the night, a giant orange harvest moon rose in the east. The season was drawing to a close and it was time to hasten south.

It was an easy passage to Padstow, dubbed "Padstein"; we breakfasted at Rick Stein's Café the following day, cycled up the railway to buy a bottle of Camel Valley Bacchus Dry and enjoyed it later with risotto on board (with prawns from Stein's fishmonger, of course).

Food had been another feature of our grand tour. We mostly ate aboard, with Anne conjuring meals onto the table almost before the anchor chain had stopped rattling. My contributions were generally slower. I had

3

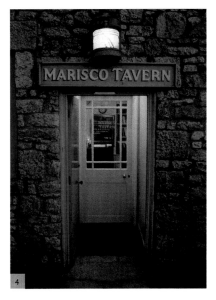

4

5

1. Leaving Bristol (credit: *Sol Purpose*)

2. Two week old seal pup on Lundy Island

3. *Nova* at anchor in Landing Bay

4. Open 24/7 and welcomes visiting sailors

5. Camel Valley Bacchus Dry (by bike)

1. Padstow Harbour

2. Longships Lighthouse,
Land's End (1875)

gained respect for fishermen and chefs, discovering the hard way how long it takes to transform a generous donation of live crabs into a delicate supper.

Turning the corner of England, we were thankful for gentle conditions again. Our friends on yacht *Shearwater* had battled their way out of Padstow a few weeks earlier. In contrast, we cruised gently downwind along the north Cornish coast, zigzagging to stop the awkward rolling. I calculated we could be at the Scilly Isles by evening, but the weather was closing in so we opted for the Wra, Botallack Head, Cape Cornwall and the Armed Knight at Land's End en route to Newlyn for the night. Now we were on the historic route taken by ships throughout history as they approached England from the west. With a sense of being on the final stretch of our journey we tacked through deep swells off the Lizard, reached past waiting tankers anchored in 80 m-deep waters, and entered the last of our 12 Ports: Falmouth.

PILOT BOOKS
Bristol Channel Yachting
   Association – The Blue Book
   (Yachting and Cruising
   Guide to the Bristol
   Channel)

ONLINE/APPS
 www.visitmyharbour.com
 www.eOceanic.com

▶ *Pendennis Castle (1542)*

WILD PROMISE OF THE WESTERN OCEAN
PHILIP MARSDEN

UNTIL LATE IN the 16th century, the port of Falmouth did not exist. On the site where it would emerge, from where it has since grown to a town of well over 20,000, stood a single building – a limekiln. Over the coming centuries, as the oceans became the conduit for Europe's expanding appetites, the buildings around the limekiln multiplied, the masts in the waters below grew thicker and a bustling port appeared.

Victualling, repairs and shelter were what it offered. But its principal business was communications. Falmouth was a packet port. From its quays, messages and documents sped around the world in vessels that could outsail all but the quickest of privateers. Bullion came back, the surplus of Britain's trade, and was transported overland to London under armed guard. As sail gave way to steam in the mid-19th century, Falmouth's importance diminished. Its natural advantages counted for less; its old vitality began to dissipate. Its story neatly spans the period in which wind-driven shipping transformed the world, the distant places of the earth began to be connected and the atlas formed into the familiar mosaic of nation states.

Falmouth is a magnificent natural harbour. Deep and sheltered, its waters have always provided succour for shipping. Out in the far west of Britain, with the Lizard peninsula breaking the Atlantic

Out in the far west of Britain, with the Lizard peninsula breaking the Atlantic swells, Falmouth was the first port of call for ocean-weary vessels

swells, it was the first port of call for ocean-weary vessels, and the last harbour for those heading down across the Bay of Biscay and around the world. But the estuary was vulnerable. Any settlement close to its mouth was exposed to raiders. Villages on the coast were frequently pillaged. Until the reign of Henry VIII, the main port on the Fal was a mile or so upstream from Falmouth, at Penryn, where a chain was stretched across the narrow river for protection.

That all changed with the building of Pendennis Castle in 1542, and its twin across the estuary, at St Mawes. Henry's dispute with Rome had exposed him to a military threat from the continent. His defending of England's south coast included fortifying the Fal. The land for Pendennis was leased from a family called Killigrew and they became the castle's keepers. With a little martial might behind them, the Killigrews grew rapidly in wealth and power. They were part of a zealous Protestant ascendancy. Opportunistic and bold, they exerted control over the waters of the Fal, drawing its passing ships into what would become Falmouth's inner harbour. They enlarged their house at Arwenack (you can still see something of its semi-ruined grandeur near the National Maritime Museum Cornwall). Various members of the family went to London and became part of Elizabeth's West Country contingent (she was said to speak a little Cornish). The wives of Henry Killigrew and William Cecil, England's most powerful man, were sisters.

But the sea has its temptations – something

Elizabeth herself, the "pirate queen", was not immune to. Down in Cornwall, the Killigrews helped themselves to cargoes in their own growing port. By the time of the Armada, the head of the family – John Killigrew, Vice Admiral of Cornwall – ran a semi-autonomous fief, roaming the county with a posse of armed followers: "he kept not within the compass of any law," complained one charge-sheet. A decade later, the rumours spread: he was ready to turn Pendennis Castle, and thereby the Fal estuary, to the Spanish. Another Armada was on its way, and the Spanish plan was – with Pendennis Castle in their hands – to use the Fal as a base from which to press on and conquer England overland. They were only prevented by the weather – the "anti-Catholic winds" – which shifted to the north-east and prevented the invading fleet from reaching the Cornish coast. John Killigrew was arrested. He died in Fleet prison, in London, deeply in debt.

Such was the dubious milieu from which Falmouth grew. But it wasn't so different from that of England itself. When Elizabeth came to the throne in 1558, the country was isolated. Much of Europe was hostile to it. The "navy" consisted of just 21 ships. Only one person in England was capable at that time of sailing a ship to the equator. But within half a century, the rogue state had asserted its place on the world stage, and its confidence on the sea had led to a flowering of distant and lucrative colonies.

The port of Falmouth resembled a colony itself. Open to the sea, its population was all settlers, its territory "virgin". Only the Killigrews had vested interests and those were now being picked over by incoming entrepreneurs. With the imprisonment of John Killigrew, control of Pendennis Castle was lost to the family, and the monopolies of their fiefdom dissolved.

In 1688 Falmouth became a packet port, and throughout the 18th century it continued to offer its natural assets to shipping – commercial, civic and naval. It played its part in the wars with the French, housing the Western Fleet for a while. Its wharves and its town houses were full of a certain sort of character, dreamers and chancers, for whom the sea and its traffic provided freedom and opportunity.

Tolerance was one result and the town was a haven for minorities and religious dissenters. There was a small but busy Jewish community. The Quaker clan of Foxes settled and became the principal shipping agents for a couple of centuries. Baptists, Congregationalists and Independents all built houses of prayer. They were joined by the New Independents, Irvingites, Rechabites and Unitarians. It was said in the 18th century that of all the towns

John Killigrew, Vice Admiral of Cornwall, ran a semi-autonomous fief, roaming the county with a posse of armed followers

Falmouth was a packet port. From its quays, messages and documents sped around the world in vessels that could outsail all but the quickest privateers

in Britain, Falmouth had "a greater proportion of persons adhering to different religious sects".

For hundreds of years, Falmouth provided ships with the chance to avoid having to tack down the English Channel, exposing themselves to the attentions of the French. With the advent of steam power, and the coming of the railways, Falmouth no longer offered an advantage. In the mid-19th century, it lost its packet service to Liverpool and Southampton.

> *More recently, there has been something of a revival in the town's fortunes*

Since then, its fortunes have been mixed. Turn-of-the-century hotels sprouted along its southern beaches; tourists basked in its mild climate. It continued as a repair port. The early establishment of the polytechnic, in 1833, was a measure of the town's lively spirit of scientific inquiry. Falmouth School of Art was set up in 1902. But the 20th century was a period of slow decline, with high unemployment and dwindling activity in the shadow of its more prosperous past. Revitalising schemes appeared every now and then. In the 1930s, it was suggested as a main port for transatlantic passengers (Southampton was eventually chosen). It would be a container port (too far from markets), or a cruise ship terminal (damaging capital dredging required).

More recently, there has been something of a revival in the town's fortunes. The estuary is a destination for walkers, leisure boaters and tens of thousands of annual visitors who wander its creeks and villages, its coastal paths. Falmouth Docks are busy with repair, refuelling and service contracts.

Pendennis Shipyard is a successful builder and refitter of international superyachts, employing a highly skilled workforce. The town has also been invigorated by Falmouth University, bringing several thousand students and staff to the area. In their diversity and the ferment of ideas is an echo of Falmouth's years as a packet port.

Just above the Prince of Wales Pier is an open area that serves as something of a centre for the town. A granite obelisk rises from the middle, inscribed with the legend: *To the Memory of the Gallant Officers and Men of H M Post Office and Packet Service sailing from Falmouth 1688–1852.* Buses turn around it. Taxis queue nearby. Few people know it's there. The area is called the Moor, which in Cornwall refers to any area of boggy ground. Underneath the tarmac is an old watercourse, which until a few centuries ago seeped down through mud and carr to the sea below. Just beside it, where the library and art gallery now stand, was the original limekiln.

PHILIP MARSDEN

Philip Marsden is the award-winning author of a number of works of travel, fiction and non-fiction, including Rising Ground, The Bronski House, The Spirit-Wrestlers *and* The Levelling Sea. *His most recent book,* The Summer Isles: A Voyage of the Imagination *(2019), charts a single-handed sail up the west coasts of Ireland and Scotland. He is a fellow of the Royal Society of Literature and his work has been translated into 15 languages. He lives in Cornwall.*

▶ *Sailors mingle with shipping (RFA Lyme Bay, pictured 2017) in Falmouth*

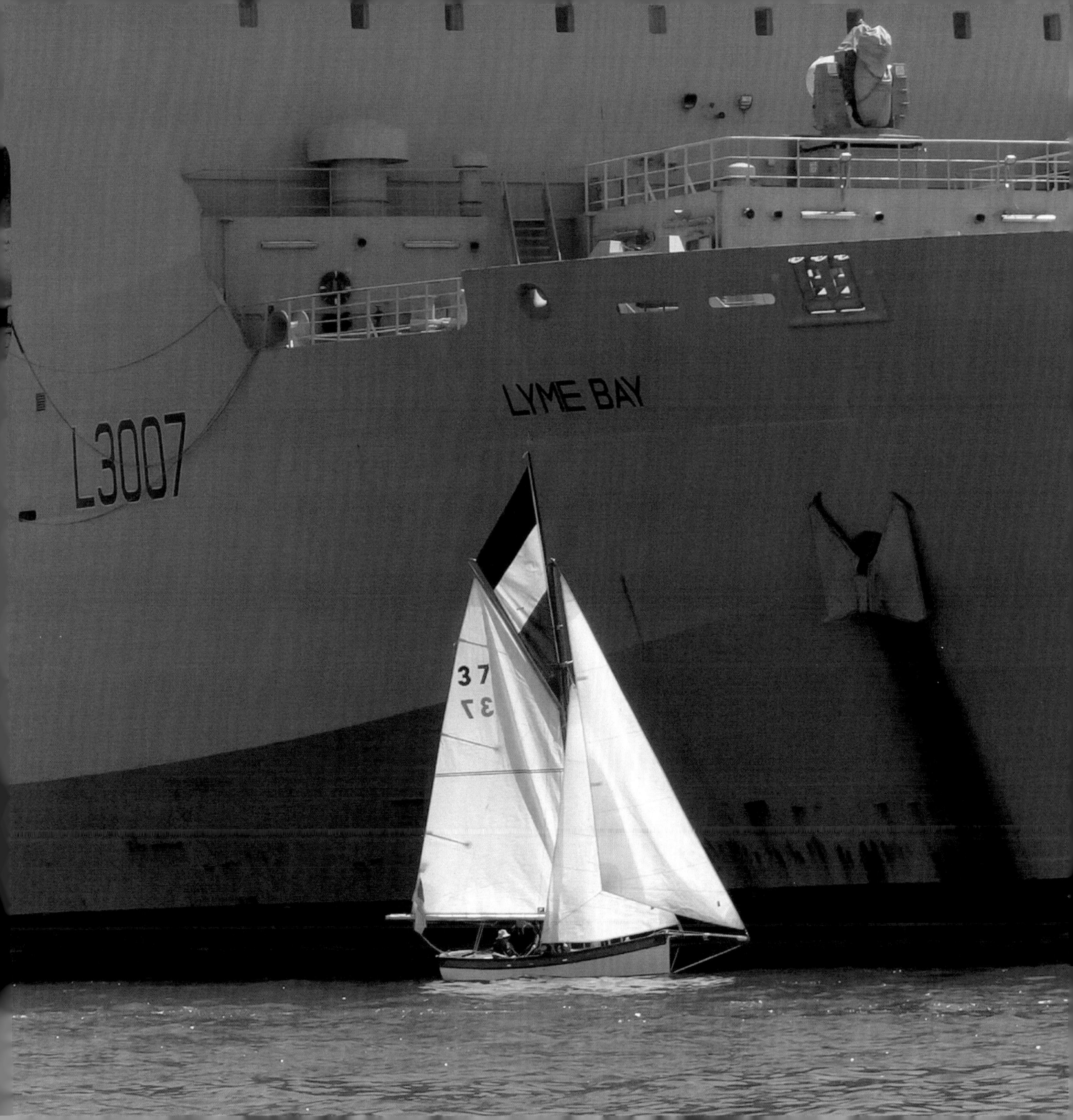
LYME BAY
L3007
37
37

RETURNING **HOME**

PASSAGE
Falmouth
to Southampton (Beaulieu)

STOPS
Plymouth
Dartmouth
Weymouth
Lymington

DISTANCE *(NM)*
181

PASSAGE TIME *(% +motor)*
32h (34%)

WIND

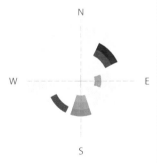

IT WAS 3 A.M. and Amanda, at the wheel of the ambulance, was heading straight for the roadblock. "Coming through," she said in a matter-of-fact tone, and drove at speed without hesitation round the barrier and across the newly laid tarmac.

The road crew had been warned we wouldn't stop. This was the only way in and out of Kingswear. I was in the passenger seat, grimly enjoying the ride, and grateful that my worst nightmare – a medical emergency – had taken place while moored up for the night at Darthaven Marina, not at sea.

Just after bed, our most senior crew member had suffered a heart attack. The symptoms were unmistakeable, so we dialled 999 immediately. We waited three long hours for the ambulance to arrive – a symptom of an overstretched service. When the paramedics finally reached us, followed by a second ambulance, it was clear that it would take more to extract one very sick person from a yacht. An hour later the volunteer coastguard team arrived from Brixham with a special stretcher. When the patient was finally extracted, I counted 11 rescuers on the pontoon. They saved his life.

Our medical drama took place on the final leg of our voyage, from Falmouth along the Cornish and Devon coast. A succession of autumn storms had arrived, and our passage eastwards consisted of dodging them. I quite enjoyed it: looking for weather windows. While in Falmouth we spotted a window over breakfast, made a quick passage plan, and departed almost immediately for Plymouth, where we were stuck again for several days. We found ourselves in the good company of the aptly named yacht *Serendipity*, also heading home to the Isle of Wight after rashly promising to sail to and from a family party… on Barra in the Outer Hebrides.

Early starts in the dark; sailing into the sunrise; dramatic skies; huge naval vessels; a French fishing fleet apparently working its way along the 12-mile limit – these were all features of the familiar coast as we sailed home in spurts. Some people would have ploughed on, bad weather or not. But we had a choice, and we opted for safe and civilised sailing. Besides, getting "stuck" was a chance to explore places we might not otherwise visit for long, like Plymouth with

1. Dartmouth waterfront
2. Atlantic storm, 27 September (Source: Windy.com)
3. Military exercises off Plymouth

its impressive naval buildings and history. For a few days, my morning jog was on Plymouth's famous Hoe.

And so, on 3 October as we approached the Needles Lighthouse, the reality of circumnavigation dawned on me. We had left the Solent heading east, and now we were approaching from the west. It was an immensely satisfying feeling. Safely, unhurriedly, sociably we had explored these islands and returned to the Beaulieu River. After 2,587 nautical miles and 155 overnight stops, our journey was complete.

PILOT BOOKS
Imray – The Shell Channel Pilot

ONLINE/APPS
www.visitmyharbour.com
www.eOceanic.com

REFLECTION

LAND OF A THOUSAND ISLANDS

"**W**HAT WAS THE highlight?" people ask. There were highlights of course, but I like to ask a different question about our voyage: "What did we discover?"

We expected to see wild and beautiful coastline. We expected to find out what it's like to live on board a boat. We expected to be tested and to learn about ourselves and each other. Anne and I were inserting a punctuation mark in the flow of our lives – a deliberate disruption between work and home projects, as well as following our own advice not to put off an adventure for too long.

Ports and trade routes are our nation's umbilical cord

We were travellers, but we were not tourists. The timing of our journey had given rise to a broader ambition. With Brexit negotiations in full flow, we planned to spend time exploring less well-known destinations – places with character, not just charisma. We wondered: might we discover a sense of unity beneath the evident divisions?

THE COMMERCIAL MARITIME WORLD

Setting out, one of the first and strongest impressions we gained was the extent and importance of the commercial maritime world. All those buoys, lights and rescue services were not primarily put in place for us, but for the ships – large and small – that ply our coastal waters day and night. Unseen to most of us, ports and their associated trade routes are our nation's umbilical cord – a symbol of our interdependence with other countries.

Later, towards the end of our journey in Falmouth, I stumbled across a portacabin labelled "The Mission to Seafarers". It turned out to be an Aladdin's cave of home comforts, practical help and a friendly ear for ships' crew – one of a network of such centres around the world. It's a cause we are proud to be supporting with this book.

MISSING AT SEA

An artist once told me that it is best to convey some subjects by painting the empty space around them. On our journey some things were conspicuous by their absence, although it took longer to notice them. For example, we saw little evidence of law enforcement, and we were only questioned twice, near London. Is that because the coast is a peaceful place? Or are efforts quietly targeted, or thinly spread?

As we moved further from London, ethnic diversity also became rarer, while at sea women are almost absent, making up just 2 per cent of the world's 1.2 million seafarers. This "empty space" first struck us as we sat at anchor in the Farne Islands, reading about the rare sea-rescuing exploits of Grace Darling in the early 1800s. It struck me again as I noticed that our "12 Ports" articles were coming in – from men.

On our journey we enjoyed meeting women breaking the mould. Wendy Stowe, harbour master at Beaulieu, helped us prepare for the voyage. Lifeboat crew and hotelier Roz Ware showed us around the Longhope lifeboat (Orkney). We were

Just 2 per cent of the world's seafarers are women

grateful to the female team member of Brixham coastguard, stretchering our crew to safety in the middle of the night. And we admired Yvonne Shields O'Connor, CEO of Irish Lights and joint author of our Dublin article, who makes a point of encouraging women into the maritime world.

A SAILOR'S IDENTITY

I thrived in the peripatetic life: carrying our home with us slowly from place to place, like a snail. In each port I imagined living and working there. Jogging in the morning to learn the streets, very quickly it felt familiar. "Could I also make a contribution here?" I asked myself. We both ended the voyage more willing to entertain the idea of living and working elsewhere.

It is surprising how strong is the grip of the labels we attach to ourselves. Taking on the identity of a sailor allowed me to interact with people in a way that was unencumbered by other roles. "We've just landed – would you tell us about this place?" was an invitation few could resist.

We listened, and looked for unifying themes. There were many maritime links between the 12 ports. The same engineers designed and built impressive Victorian breakwaters and lighthouses. The same boats passed through or were repaired, and the same ships' captains made history in these places. Captain Bligh's *Bounty* was built in Hull. Bligh then turned up in Dublin, designing solutions to their harbour silting up. *Titanic* connections were everywhere.

ISLANDS OF IDENTITY

Although looking for unifying themes, what struck me more was the sense of local identity in each place. I remember the nightwatchman in the smart yacht marina at North Shields. He had worked as a mechanic all around the world, before returning home to start a family. Glowing with native Tyneside pride, he showered praise on the world-class local hospital, schools and the nearby Northumbrian landscape. Other places were equally proud. I think of the independent people of Hull, "eight miles east of England". I loved their spirit, and grew to understand their frustrations with distant decision-making in London.

Visiting by boat, even small islands feel like independent nations. It's an impression reinforced by the scale of the coastal scenery, and exaggerated by travelling everywhere at jogging pace. In "Made of Stories" (his essay for this project), Nick Isbister encourages us to turn the map of Britain upside down and remember that Orkney was once at the centre of things. Still today it feels like a self-contained

kingdom, almost as distant from Edinburgh as it is from London.

National labels don't do justice to this. Maybe we in the UK should think of ourselves less as two islands or four nations, and more as a rich, diverse "archipelago"? Then we might focus on the resilience that exists in a network of local communities, and allow ourselves to think about the bridges and relationships we need to build between our many islands of identity, and around the world.

One common characteristic stood out: we found generous people everywhere. I'll not forget the lifeboatman in northern Scotland, helping us with an oil change and later welcoming us like honoured guests to the community barbecue; or the retired welder in Belfast, telling stories through his long dark beard and, with gnarled hands, making a small repair for nothing.

CYCLES OF HISTORY

Now, as I write this reflection, we are in the grip of a different kind of crisis. Eclipsing Brexit, the pandemic will be followed – with the inevitability of an outgoing tide – by economic recession. Many of the places we visited have seen this before. When fishing and shipbuilding declined, some rebuilt their economies around oil and gas.

Today many have grand plans to succeed through tourism, green technology or other forms of enterprise. As we enter a new era, it remains to be seen whether these plans succeed, and whether "levelling up" reaches them all.

Resilience is in the history of these places

Whatever comes, resilience is in the history of these places.

LESSONS FOR SAILORS

Our own "grand plan" succeeded by holding the vision lightly. Mentally we were both prepared to halt the voyage at any time if circumstances changed, or if one of us didn't want to carry on. It would have been disappointing, but I was philosophical and positive about that. Ambition is healthy, but fixed plans don't go well with sailing, nor with partnerships or teams. Decisions were made jointly.

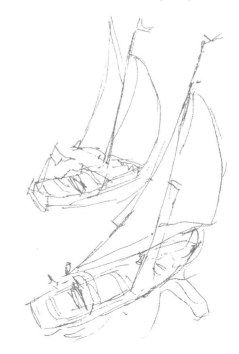

There were practical sailing truths to be learned or reconfirmed too, which other circumnavigators may find useful:

You won't need as many clothes as you think. But it's cold: we wore thermals daily until July. You will discover it's true that seasickness lessens with time at sea, but it will come and surprise you when you are tired and least expect it. You may not admit it, but you and your crew will feel afraid – the necessary fear that comes from experience, or inexperience, or both. You will also have easy sailing, and you will delight in using your biggest sail more than you expect. You might discover, as we did, that hot cross buns are the best sailing snack ever. You will obsess over squeaky ropes and fenders; we refined the art of deploying dynamic climbing ropes. You will puzzle over weather apps for hours (Windguru? Meteoconsult?) before concluding that your most reliable guide is the BBC Coastal Forecast. You will establish a rhythm, and grow in confidence as a sailor.

And when you have done all that, and day has followed day, and the miles have ticked past, an hour will come when the meaning of circumnavigation will suddenly surprise you, as it did me. There are still a thousand places we didn't visit, but we had encircled them all. Now when I hear the mention of a place, it brings memories. The weather forecast brings emotions. And with fresh amazement and a new sense of gratitude, I can call this archipelago "home".

You will feel the necessary fear... and you will also have easy sailing

AROUND THESE ISLANDS
The archipelago of Great Britain and Ireland is said to include about 4,400 islands, counting those that are 0.2 hectares or more at all states of tide. Of these, 850 are in the Republic of Ireland, and about 210 inhabited (70 in ROI).

▶ Longhope, Orkney